# a little piece of earth

# a little piece of earth

## how to grow your own food in small spaces

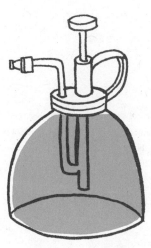

## maria finn

*illustrations by* **eika**

universe

First published in the United States of America in 2010
by Universe Publishing,
A Division of Rizzoli International Publications, Inc.
300 Park Avenue South
New York, NY 10010
www.rizzoliusa.com

2010  2011  2012  2013  /  10  9  8  7  6  5  4  3  2  1

Design by Sara E. Stemen
Printed in the United States of America

Printed on 100% recycled paper with soy-based inks.
ISBN: 978-0-7893-2027-8
Library of Congress Control Number: 2009939875

for my grandparents

mark and vivian stevermer

# contents

# introduction

Nobody is born a gardener. It's a slow, steady development, wrought with tribulations and triumphs, frustration, and moments of grace. Over the past few decades the simple, miraculous process of growing our own food has fallen by the wayside as technology allowed us faster, more convenient ways of living. But now there's a return to edible gardening. Not only does growing produce improve one's diet, but gardening is good exercise itself as it burns just over 300 calories an hour. Along with the physical health benefits, it promotes a spectrum of well-being. You can find relaxation in your garden after work, touching and smelling something beautiful. The garden also encourages a philosophical approach to understanding and accepting the cycles of life. Growing vegetables brings people back to a simpler more sustainable time—not to mention saving on food bills. Gardening can be calming or energizing, a solitary or group activity. As well, growing and then serving the perfect tomatoes gives one bragging rights.

The Grow Your Own movement is gaining momentum and not always in the traditional places. Fruits and vegetables are now found on front yards where lawns have been ripped up and replaced by rows of chard, kale, and other leafy greens. They are on rooftops, floating barges, the beds of pick-up trucks, and in junker cars.

The sorry state of school lunches has inspired educators to start gardening programs so that children have hands-on courses in science and nutrition through their schoolyards. But growing food is not just for the young. Senior citizens and handicapped people are increasingly included in the design of gardens.

Memories can be found in fig and almond trees, or in the scents of lavender and rosemary. These days there are corn stalks in alleyways, and tubers in raised beds on garage roofs. There are wild fruit trees and foraged leafy greens picked by resourceful foodies who aren't stopped by the fact that they may not own their own green space. You can make lavender and honey ice cream by harvesting flowers from your herb pots, have fresh salad greens almost year-round from a space as small as a windowbox, and grow specialty strawberries in arm's reach of your kitchen.

*A Little Piece of Earth* can be a starting point for beginners, or, for more experienced gardeners, it may give suggestions for different heirlooms to try. There are lots of design ideas for space-saving techniques and many fun and easy projects. With each new herb, leafy green, fruit tree, or vegetable bed, your quality of life will improve, and you'll experience a newfound pleasure. Edible gardeners soon find themselves part of an obsessed community, and gain a sense of pride when cooking and making drinks with specialty, seasonal produce picked from their own plots. Edible gardens not only provide food, but also connections—to the earth, to the past, to culture, and to one another.

—MARIA FINN

*Chapter* **1** **OUT ON A LEDGE**
INDOOR AND
WINDOWBOX EDIBLES

The American tradition of self-reliance has increasingly dwindled to the point that "subsistence living" means a drawer full of take-out menus and some bottled drinking water near at hand. But growing your own fruit and vegetables is not just for those lucky enough to have a backyard. You can cultivate fragrant herbs in a sunny spot in your kitchen. Windowboxes planted with edibles can save you trips to the grocery store for salad greens and strawberries. Indoors, fruit trees, like kumquats, Meyer lemons, bananas, and even orchids that create vanilla pods, make fragrant and beautiful houseplants that also provide fruit. Dark corners are the perfect spot for cultivating specialty mushrooms. This chapter explores edible possibilities for the seriously space-challenged.

# Worm Composting

It all begins with the soil. Worms are great transformers of the landscape through their eating and digesting. They can consume a patch of stones and over time turn it into a fertile field. Worms continually pass soil through their intestinal canals, keep anything they can use for food, and then "cast" the rest. With an indoor worm composter, these creatures can take your coffee grinds, lettuce scraps, and apple cores and turn them into fertilizer castings that your plants will love.

Worm composting is easy and serves two purposes. The first is reducing the amount of organic waste that goes into our landfills, and the second is creating wonderful nitrogen-rich humus for your plants. It's also fun to show off your 2,000 red worms to guests. When telling them about the "juice" that comes out of the bottom of the composter, I like to keep a straight face while explaining that it's really good for your hair and nails. Some friends have seemed resistant to eating at my place after that.

The last book written by Charles Darwin was a slim volume on earthworms titled *The Formation of Vegetable Mould Through the Actions of Worms with Observations on their Habits*. Darwin made close notes on the earthworm's physiology, habits, and even eating preferences. It seems, Darwin learned, that the earthworm is a super-taster, preferring the subtle flavors of cabbage, turnip, celery, and carrot to more robust mint, sage, and thyme. These observations are good to keep in mind when sorting your scraps.

See the Resources at the end of the book to find out where to order worms and compost bins. As well, keep in mind that many cities have classes on worm composting and offer subsidized or free composters.

To start with, I keep a small stainless steel container with a carbon filter in its lid next to my sink for scraps. The carbon filter ensures that no odors escape. Particularly early on, try to choose vegetables for your worms that are nonacidic, such as salad greens rather than onions. Eggshells that have been ground up, tea bags, and coffee grinds can go into the mix. Later, when the worms become heartier eaters, you can increase the volume and variety of vegetables and fruit that you feed them, but avoid oily foods, clippings from house-plants, and any animal matter. I also try to feed mine only organic produce so that there are no traces of pesticides in their food.

Any lidded plastic container with airholes punched into the upper half of the box or lid will work as a worm composter. However, try to avoid some of the debacles that friends of mine have experienced with worm composting: One friend forgot to put airholes in her plastic box and smothered her worms to death. Another didn't have a firm lid and left the composter near the clothes dryer in the laundry room. After the heat triggered a mass exodus from the compost box, she had to collect thousands of red worms by hand.

You can instead purchase a multitiered worm composter from a local garden supply or hardware store. Along with the air holes and firm lids, I find that the layered composter makes it easier and cleaner to harvest the castings and the worm juice. When you order your worms (see page 207), you'll need a minimum of 1,000 red worms to start with, and if you have a large commercially built composter, start with 2,000 worms. It sounds like a lot, but it's not. The worms will reproduce until you have 20,000 worms, but they will not overpopulate.

When adding worm compost to your houseplants, sprinkle castings over the top layer of the soil. Each time you water, the compost feeds the houseplants. But because with regular watering, the nutrients drain out of the soil quickly, be sure to fertilize with worm compost often.

Different worm composters will come with instructions and bedding, but here are a few basic steps for getting started.

STEP 1: Drill or poke airholes into your plastic container. Make sure to choose a container that is deep enough— at least a foot deep.

STEP 2: Prepurchased composters come with bedding, but if you want to make your own, use shredded newspaper, cardboard, sawdust, or even pieces of straw. (Some instructions will tell you to use manure, but I avoid this in case the animals were given any deworming medication.)

STEP 3: Empty the worms into the tray. Since they don't like sunlight, they will quickly dive down into the matter if you leave the lid opened and expose them to light for a few moments. Then cover them with dampened newspaper.

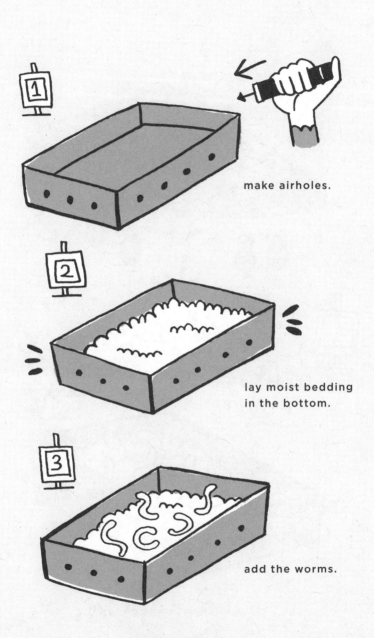

1. make airholes.

2. lay moist bedding in the bottom.

3. add the worms.

WORM COMPOSTING

place kitchen scraps on top.

If you don't have room for a worm composter, many community gardens and farmer's markets will accept your compostable garbage and give you a little compost in exchange.

STEP 4: Place a few handfuls of your kitchen scraps on top of the newspaper. If you chop the scraps into smaller pieces, it will be easier for the worms to eat. Then cover the food with more damp newspaper. (It shouldn't be soaking wet, just damp.) As a rule of thumb, you shouldn't have more than an inch of food covering half the surface area. You are overfeeding your worms if you find black flies in your compost bin.

Within about 3 months, the worms will turn much of the kitchen waste into rich worm castings ready to use with your plants. You can mix the castings into your potting soil, and then keep adding the castings in layers over the soil in your planters. As you water, the nutrients will drain into the soil.

## Potting Soil

Almost all garden centers sell excellent potting soil mixtures enhanced with everything from bat guano to seaweed. Since you are planting things you will eat, don't skimp and buy organic. There are many different ways to mix your own potting soil, but the main components you want are elements that keep the soil lightweight and well drained, including vermiculite or perlite. The soil also needs an element that will hold moisture—peat moss or humus. This is important because pots tend to dry out faster than the ground, and the smaller the pot,

OVERWATERING—YELLOWING LEAVES

UNDERWATERING—SHRIVELED LEAVES

the faster it dries out. Worm castings also provide humus that helps retain moisture. The more you water, the more you will need to add nutrients, as these drain out of the soil. To make your own potting soil, mix together equal amounts of rich, organic soil, vermiculite or perlite, and worm castings.

I'd be willing to bet that more plants die from overwatering than underwatering. In some houses everyone who passes by a plant—the babysitter, a new boyfriend or girlfriend, and grandparents—feels the need to dump a glass of water on it. A plant with yellowing leaves is probably being loved to death. A plant that looks like it is shriveling is probably being neglected. An inexpensive and handy purchase is a watering meter that tells you how moist or dry the soil is. You can also plug a finger down into the dirt. There is no one answer for how much water a plant needs—this depends on the size of your pots and the material within the pots. Be sure to have a small drainage tray under each pot to catch runoff water, but your plants should also never be sitting in water as this will cause their roots to rot. Usually indoor plants need to be watered once a week, with a good, even soaking.

Prepare or "season" your water by leaving a full watering can out overnight so that the chlorine and other chemicals can evaporate from it before you use it on your houseplants.

CLOCHES AND TERRARIUMS

## Starting Seeds in Cloches and Terrariums

You can grow the most interesting heirlooms and other varieties by starting your plants from seeds rather than purchasing them as starts from a nursery. You probably remember those little egg carton planter projects in grade school. That's really how simple it is. Add dirt, press a seed in, and remember to water. Garden supply stores and many hardware stores sell seed-starter kits with little pellets of humus and clear plastic trays to cover them and create a greenhouse effect. However, if you are gardening in a small space, like indoors or on your windowsill, then you don't need tons of plants from a seed-starter kit. It is often a rather large plastic container, and I consider it something of an eyesore to have in the house.

Instead, try starting seeds in something that looks attractive. To cultivate small amounts of salad greens indoors, for instance, you can use Edwardian terrariums made of glass and metal or a large cloche with a saucer. These have the same greenhouse effect as the plastic kits, yet they look nice in your living space. Salad greens grow quickly from seeds. Herbs, especially the woodier ones like rosemary, are an exception. They are much more slow growing so it's worth it to just buy them as starts.

For smaller starts, get very small, clean terra-cotta planters with drainage holes in the bottom. Fill them with good potting soil and plant a few seeds in each one. To intensify the heat and light, put them under a cloche (or a bell-shaped glass), or inside a glass terrarium. This arrangement will look very nice and could go in the center of a table if it's in a sunny spot. Keep the seedlings moist. When they start to sprout, remove the glass cover. If there are too many plants growing up against each other, cull out the spindlier ones. After each plant has a few leaves, fertilize them with worm castings.

If the seedlings are going to be outdoor plants, they will need to be hardened off, so put them outside on mild days and bring them back in at night. Do this for a few weeks before transplanting them into your windowbox.

Save your cloche, terrarium, and small terra-cotta containers for the next round of seeds, or plant small, tropical houseplants in the pots and keep them under the glass as a centerpiece.

# Planting in Windowboxes

You can grow fruit and delicious greens for salads on your windowsill in almost all regions of the United States and throughout most of the year. To start, measure your windows and figure out how you will attach the boxes—do you have a bar for them to hang on? A ledge they can sit on? Write out your measurements, and then shop for boxes. Make sure your windowboxes have drainage. This means that either they are wrought iron and cocomat lined, or if they are wood or aluminum, they need to have drain holes in the bottom so water can escape and the roots don't soak and drown. You can drill three evenly spaced holes in the bottom of your windowbox, then cut a piece of landscaper cloth and line the bottom of the box with it, so that dirt doesn't spill out of the drainage holes when watering. After lining the bottom, add a little drainage material, such as a ¼-inch layer of pebbles. Add another layer of lining, then fill the box with potting soil until it's about three-fourths full, then place your starts in the soil, and add more around them until they are almost level with the rim of the box. Water well and add more soil if necessary. (Often potting soil compacts after watering).

Herbs are almost always modest looking in contrast to flowers, fruits, and vegetables, but their benefits are many and their subtle beauty and charm quickly win you over. Each plant not only provides the essential flavor to favorite dishes, but it also has its own lore. During the spread of the Roman Empire, soldiers planted lavender throughout Europe. They used it to scent the air and bath-water, for cooking, and as a disinfectant of wounds and burns. In Shakespeare's *Hamlet*, confused and sad Ophelia picked rosemary so Hamlet would remember her: "... here's rosemary,

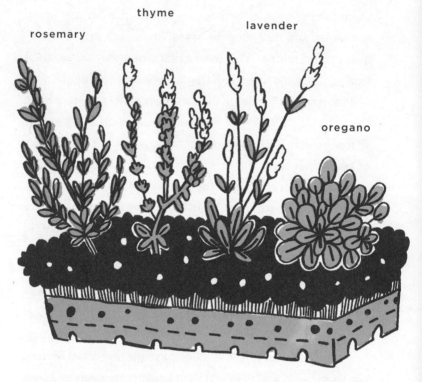

rosemary

thyme

lavender

oregano

soil with crushed shells

MEDITERRANEAN WINDOWBOX

that's for remembrance; pray love, remember." In medieval times, herbs were cultivated in castle walls by royalty and used as remedies and spices; the peasants outside the walls picked them to flavor soups and stop the fermentation of their food.

Despite their many practical and poetic functions, buying cut herbs from the store can be so frustrating because we normally only use a few leaves at a time, then stash the rest of the clump in the fridge, only to wilt and turn brown before they are finished up. This problem—along with how beautiful they look in my kitchen—has prompted me to grow indoor herbs year-round. Since you rarely rely on flowers for fresh herbs, you don't need pollinators, just a sunny window.

Traditional Mediterranean herbs should be grouped together as they like the soil a little drier. In a large container, plant lavender, thyme, rosemary, and oregano all together or each in its own smaller container lined up next to each other. These beautiful herbs will have a cool palette of blue, silver, and green. They need full sun, so put them in a south-facing window. They can take a little drying out, so you don't need to water every day, but when you do water—about three times a week, depending on how dry and hot your home is—soak the soil thoroughly. A crushed oyster shell can be added to the soil mix for extra calcium and so they feel a bit more, well, Mediterranean.

pinch here.

BASIL

## A Pot of Basil

I plant basil separately from the other Mediterranean herbs as
it tends to like more water. Basil also does well indoors in a
sunny window. You can harvest your basil and pinch it back at
the same time. Pinching leaves helps it grow fuller and bushier,
rather than thin and spindly. Pinch from the top of the plant,
where the leaves meet the stem—this place is unfortunately
called "the crotch."

# Basil or Oregano Ice Cubes

If you have a bumper crop of basil or oregano, make herb ice cubes. Frozen herbs retain their flavor much more than dried herbs and don't have that musty aftertaste. Buy an ice tray designed to make small to medium cubes. Take 3–5 basil leaves and dice them finely. Fit these into the cube section and add a small amount of water. Do the same with the oregano. When making sauces or stews, just pop out an herb ice cube and add it to the pot. (Note: Rosemary and thyme do not seem to freeze as well.)

# Rosemary and Thyme-Infused Vodka

Start with a premium, clean-tasting vodka. I like to use Tito's Handmade Vodka made in Austin, Texas. Rinse 1 sprig of rosemary and 2 sprigs of thyme. Put these into a clean Mason jar. Pour 750 ml. of vodka over the herbs, screw the lid on, and shake the jar a few times. Then store it in a cool, dark place for two days. Taste the flavor of the infusion. If you'd like it stronger, leave it a few days longer. Once the vodka suites your taste, strain the herbs from it using a filter. Wash the jar and put the vodka back into it. These make great martinis garnished with an herb sprig and a twist of lemon.

As for varieties, 'Sweet Green' is the classic for Italian cooking, but expand your horizons and try the Thai basil 'Siam Queen' for a unique licorice taste. 'Red Rubin' is both fragrant and beautiful with deep-purple-red leaves, and 'Cinnamon Basil' has violet stems and a hint of the spice in its flavor.

## Strawberry Windowbox

In medieval times strawberries symbolized prosperity, peace, and perfection. Through history they have also been considered an aphrodisiac, and some lore has it that when Native Americans taught the settlers how to sweeten cornbread with strawberries, this was the inception of the strawberry shortcake. What is undisputed about strawberries is that they have no fat, very few calories, and are rich in vitamin C, potassium, folic acid, fiber, and vitamin B6. And very few things taste better than a perfectly ripened strawberry.

Primarily, people grow three different kinds of strawberries: June-bearing strawberries produce one large crop in early summer. These are the biggest berries; their root system is on runners so the plants spread easily. The other two, everbearing and day-neutral strawberries, produce berries from spring into fall. They are smaller berries than June-bearing strawberries, but still very sweet. If you have a shadier spot, you can try growing Alpine strawberries, a wild European variety that is small, but it is a pretty plant and the fruit has a nice flavor.

To plant strawberries add a good nitrogen-rich fertilizer to your soil—worm castings work. Plant the strawberry starts at the soil level—don't bury the stems or expose the roots. Put them about 4 inches apart in your windowbox. Water them well after planting and keep the soil moist to the touch.

Fresh strawberries are wonderful for plucking and putting in yogurt in the morning or on top of ice cream after dinner. But the real advantage to growing your own strawberries is that on commercial, nonorganic farms large amounts of pesticides are sprayed to grow strawberries; in fact, they are one of the most pesticide-laden fruit found on grocery store shelves. According to the Environmental Working Group website, pesticides were found on 90 percent of the strawberries tested.

## Salad Windowbox

The planting suggestions offered here are based on window-boxes that are 36 inches long and include 5 plants each. Space the plants evenly in the box. I like the appearance of full, crowded boxes, but if you'd like to give yours more room, then add fewer plants.

During peak summer months lettuces can tend to "bolt" or grow upright and develop a bitter taste and tough texture (see page 114), so plan a box for spring or early summer, and then sow new seeds or add new starts to replant for an autumn salad box. Mix varied colors and leaf textures in your boxes for aesthetics. The different greens will also have a variety of textures and flavors to make an interesting salad composed of just greens. Some greens, such as arugula and escarole, tend to be bitter, those in the mustard family are spicy, and others, like romaine and butter lettuces, are sweeter and mild. A little chervil adds a nice hint of anise to your salad.

To harvest the greens, just pick off the outer leaves when they are young and tender—there's no need to cut the entire plant. Here are some suggestions:

In the early summer plant red-leaf lettuce, little gem lettuce, freckles romaine, rocket arugula, and frisé. This windowbox can take some dappled shade, but it should get about 6 hours of sun a day in cooler temperatures. Keep the soil moist to the touch.

In really hot, sunny places, your greens won't be happy in peak summer, so put some herbs or flowers in the box for July and August. If you live in a cool place or have partial shade, go ahead with your autumn replanting a little earlier. Plant your box with tatsoi, escarole, mâche, spinach, and chard for an early winter salad box.

One of my clients in New York City, Catherine Gund, a documentary filmmaker, lives with her four children and partner in one of the few remaining lofts in SoHo that is designated for artists. We installed a small vegetable and fruit garden in their windowboxes of cucumbers, tomatoes, carrots, salad greens, herbs, runner beans, raspberries, and strawberries. A few surprises have surfaced, such as a cantaloupe, which, they figure, must have come from seeds in the worm compost. Her children have the drill down: After dinner they sort out the scraps good for worm composting and put those into the bin. (One of her children ate a worm on a dare.) The kids then use the worm castings as fertilizer in the windowboxes. They have dubbed the boxes their organic farm, and pluck nasturtium, strawberries, and cherry tomatoes for snacks, and make pesto with the basil. The windowboxes for growing greens couldn't keep up, so each year we add a little more lettuce.

## Indoor Citrus Trees

When winter comes to Italy, the lemon trees potted in terracotta planters get moved indoors. Almost every large estate has a sunny, ventilated room to store their lemons, known as a *limonaia*. Winter is when the trees bloom. I've always imagined a room full of these—exquisite to the point of intoxicating. Worried about cold snaps, I've brought my pink lemon tree indoors where the smell of the blossoms on just one tree greets me every time I walk in the house. Sweeter citrus trees, like oranges and tangerines, need more heat, but acidic ones, like lemons, limes, and kumquats, do very well inside. My favorites for keeping in sunny windows are Meiwa kumquat, Kaffir lime, and probably the most popular indoor fruit tree, the dwarf Improved Meyer lemon.

When ordering your tree, find out how large it will be. They are usually sold by their age or container size. Purchase

PRESERVED LEMONS

# Preserved Lemons

These are great chopped up and used as a condiment with Indian and Morrocan dishes, or with grilled fish. If you want to make them Moroccan style, add cloves, cardamom, peppercorns, a cinnamon stick, and bay leaf.

* ½ cup kosher salt
* 8–10 Meyer lemons
* Quart-sized Mason jar (sterilized)

**1** Put about $1/_2$ inch of salt in the bottom of a clean and sterilized Mason jar.

**2** Scrub the lemons clean and cut $1/_4$ inch off the tip of each lemon. You want to almost quarter the lemons lengthwise while keeping them attached at the base. Pry them open and coat the insides and outsides with salt.

**3** Then fill the jar with the lemons, packing them in tightly so that their juices are released and fill the jar. If there isn't enough juice, add some extra freshly squeezed juice. Add the remaining salt. Seal the jar and let it sit at room temperature for a couple days. Every once in a while turn it over and shake it very gently. The rinds will need about three weeks to soften. You can store these in the refrigerator for about 6 months. Before serving, discard any seeds still caught in there, and wash well to rinse off the excess salt. (I also love blood oranges preserved in this way.)

one that's 2–3 years old (the tree should be at least 3 feet high by then), and plant it in a container only 2 inches larger than the root-ball.

For a citrus tree, instead of putting pebbles or other drainage materials in the bottom of the container, use a nutrient-rich draining soil mix. Then place a saucer with pebbles under the plant and add some water to the saucer. This way the roots aren't soaking, but the plant gets moisture from the evaporating water. Fill the planter about three-fourths full with the potting soil. Remove the citrus tree from its nursery pot and gently massage its roots so they can spread more easily. Place the plant into the pot and then fill in around it with more soil. Press down around the base of the plant. Don't cover the trunk with soil or leave any roots exposed. After planting, water thoroughly.

Indoor citrus trees like to be misted with water regularly. I tend to mist all my indoor plants when it rains outside so they don't feel like they're missing anything. If you live in a dry climate, mist more often. To water, use your meter and keep the soil moist to dry.

Though many citrus trees are self-pollinating, when these plants are indoors you can help the process along by hand pollinating. With a small paintbrush or Q-tip, dab lightly at the center of one flower and then another and another. (See the illustration on page 30.)

The dwarf Improved Meyer lemon is not a true lemon, but rather a hybrid from China of a true lemon and a mandarin orange. Some people miss the supertart taste of a real lemon, but many enjoy the milder flavor and the fact that the skin is slightly sweet. It can flower twice a year, so it is rarely without flowers or fruit. When the flowers turn to buds, there will be about 6 fruits in a cluster. Cull these to about two per cluster for larger lemons; leave them if you want a larger number of smaller lemons.

## KUMQUATS

Long cultivated in China and Japan, the kumquat is still a little exotic here. It's a good ornamental plant with a nice shape, lovely dark-green leaves, and tiny white flowers when in bloom. Because the flesh of the fruit is tart and the skin is sweet, the kumquat is usually eaten in one bite.

I briefly dated a music composer who was really smart but frustrated—he wanted to be hailed as a genius for his avant-garde music but had to create video game noises for a living. He had a tendency to make people angry. We went on only a few dates before I called it quits, but for some reason, he sends me a big box of fresh kumquats every year. He lives in San Jose, California, and has a large kumquat tree that produces loads of fruit, so every winter when a box arrives from San Jose, I know it's filled with the small orange fruit. I think of this gift as his yearly request for forgiveness. They are his "I'm sorry kumquats." And in the spirit they are sent, I readily accept them. In fact, I think this was my introduction to the kumquat.

KUMQUAT TREE

# Candied Kumquats

* 1 cup sugar
* 2 cups water
* ½ pound kumquats

 In a medium saucepan, bring the sugar and water to a boil, stirring until dissolved.

 Add the kumquats. Cover the fruit with a piece of parchment paper and a small plate or lid to keep them submerged.

 Simmer over low heat until the kumquats are translucent, about 25 minutes.

 Drain the fruit and reserve the syrup. Serve with anything chocolate.

I keep the tiny oval citrus in a bowl in the middle of the kitchen table and pop each one whole into my mouth. Sometimes they are toe-curling sour, but the perfect ones have a wonderful balance of sour, firm flesh, and sweet skins that mellow the taste. You eat a lot of the sour ones for that perfect one. (Maybe like kissing a lot of frogs. . . . ) But when I'm not up to the adventure of kumquat tasting, they make excellent marmalade. Make it with rosemary and not too much sugar and it's great with lamb, or it can be candied and served for dessert.

I am fascinated by my Kaffir lime tree and force almost all visitors to rub the leaves and then smell their hands. After a few seconds pass, they almost all respond along the lines of, "That's amazing." Though I realize they may just be humoring me, I like to think the marveling is sincere. The intensely fragrant leaves provide the distinctive punch in much Southeast Asian cooking, especially Thai. The fruits themselves have a rough texture and thick skin, and while many people focus on the leaves, I quite like the slightly different flavor of the juice and slice them to add to sparkling water.

## Banana Trees

A fisherman I knew in Homer, Alaska, had two banana trees growing in his living room. These tropicals had reached the ceiling, and clusters of bananas hung from them. They created a slightly surreal environment in this bachelor pad, as the floors were still bare wood—not nice wood, but the raw, rough stuff that is usually under the flooring. Bananas had fallen from the tree and were left on the wood to rot. He explained his master plan: Instead of flooring, he intended to install grass sod in his house. I suggested that he then get a goat to keep it trim for him.

Of course, sod would not do well indoors, and bananas rotting on your floor are not appealing. But if an Alaskan fisherman who is constantly heading out to sea can grow bananas, how hard can it be? Also, the tree resembles a palm and makes for a lovely ornamental.

Start with a dwarf variety, and keep in mind that the size of the pot you use will determine how big the tree gets. You can always re-pot when it seems to be too constrained. Add a little extra peat moss in with your potting soil. Put it in front of a warm, sunny window and mist occasionally, or if it's winter, you might set up a humidifier nearby. Add fertilizers high in potassium to encourage fruiting. New stalks will start to emerge—allow only one to grow, so that it can replace your main stalk after it fruits. Other suckers—or starts coming from the mother plant—can be removed to start new banana trees. Housewarming gifts for all your friends!

## Vanilla Orchids

Montezuma, the Aztec king, greeted Cortez and his army with a beverage made from the pod of an orchid that grows in Vera Cruz and the ground beans of the cacao tree. After chocolate and vanilla were brought back to Europe by the conquistadors, the world was forever changed. The Swiss made candy bars with vanilla, the Queen of England insisted it flavor her cakes, Parisians added it to perfume, Swedes blended it into cookies, a German physician dubbed it an aphrodisiac, and it just grew in popularity. The problem was trying to cultivate the plant outside of Mexico. Along with tropical temperatures, the right soil, and shade, it also needed a bee very specific to the region of Vera Cruz to pollinate it. Once this was discovered, methods for hand-pollinating vanilla were soon mastered, and now Madagascar is the number-one producer of vanilla in the world.

Growing your own vanilla is not a way to start gardening. This is for those who really want a challenge. The key to growing *V. planifolia*, the vanilla orchid, involves re-creating the Vera Cruz valley environment as much as possible. Have a pot

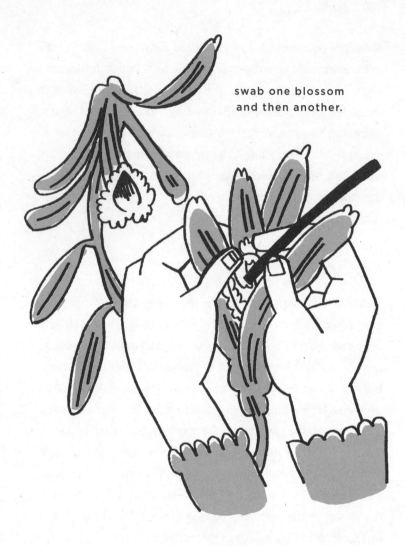

swab one blossom
and then another.

HAND POLLINATION

with really good drainage with slits in the bottom—both for water to escape and ventilation. Fill this 1/3 high with orchid mix for planting, which should include sphagnum peat moss and fir bark. Place the plant in the container, and top off the planter with more potting substance. Place the vanilla orchid in an east or west window. During the first week, instead of watering it, just mist it. When you see new growth, start watering—with a good soaking once a week—and place a pebble-filled tray underneath the pot to hold the moisture it needs.

A somewhat slow-growing vine, vanilla orchids need a structure on which to climb. Once the plant has matured, reaching the top of the support, it will cascade down and begin to flower. The beautiful orchid flowers last a day, at which time hand pollination is needed to produce the bean. The flowers will produce long, cylindrical pods about 6 months to a year later. Pick the pods and boil them in water for 30 seconds, then lay them on a towel and let them sweat for 10 days. This is how the flavor and scent are enhanced. Straighten them by hand, then dry them in the sun or on low heat in an oven until they shrink to about 1/3 of their original size.

# Mushroom Logs

The idea of heading into moist forests after a rain sounds delightful, in a "Provence, France" kind of way, but in reality you better go out with someone who really knows their fungi so you don't eat a poisonous one. One friend of mine in New York told me that when she grew up in Switzerland, her family always went mushroom hunting in the autumn. They would take their harvest to the local police station, and the officers there sorted the edible from the poisonous. She wanted us to leave the city and try this. I agreed, on the condition that she was an expert. I told her that the Brooklyn cops would not be so obliging. So if you can't hunt the mushrooms, the next best way to enjoy gourmet mushrooms is to cultivate them in your kitchen.

Wild mushrooms, such as the exotic black truffle, the sought after morel, and the much-loved porcini, are not the easiest to grow at home. In fact, I have heard mushroom hunters use the word "impossible." And though I try not to buy into that, gardening and cooking have made me more humble rather than less. The best types of mushrooms to grow at home are oysters, shitakes, white buttons, and criminis. My favorites are the oyster and the shitake.

The easiest way to begin is with a kit. This isn't the cheapest way to grow mushrooms at home, but imagine slicing fresh oyster mushrooms for a Sunday morning omelet (and impressing that significant other, no doubt) or having a shitake log as part of your kitchen décor. Once you get to know your climate and your mushroom spores, you can always get ambitious and diversify.

The health benefits of mushrooms are many: They are high in protein and rich in vitamins B and D. They help with digestion because they provide enzymes. In some Asian countries such as Japan and China, they are considered a food that promotes longevity as they have been found to lower blood pressure, protect against cancer, and contain antioxidants.

Shitake comes from the Japanese *Shii*, which means "oak" and *take*, which means "mushroom"—it literally is a piece of oak with mushrooms growing on it. Approaches to cultivating and harvesting shitake logs will depend on your temperament and budget more than anything. Are you impatient or feel like splurging? Then buy a log already prepared. Can you wait months for your mushrooms to begin? If so, follow these instructions.

STEP 1: To cultivate a shitake log, you want to use oak logs 3–6 inches in diameter and 2–3 feet long, cut between fall and spring when the sap content is highest. City dwellers can look out for neighborhood oaks when they're being pruned, or ask at the parks department. Or ask a friend with a country house, order a log online, or try to purchase one from your local farmer's market mushroom seller. In order not to partake in wounding a live oak, you can also ask an arborist if he or she will be cutting an oak down soon. Drill 1-inch-deep holes in the log. Make circles of holes around the log 6 inches apart, and space the rings 1½–2 inches apart. You can alternate the pattern so it's less symmetrical, but keep the spacing.

STEP 2: Purchase shitake spawn from a supplier listed in the Resources section (see page 209) and insert one into each

# SHITAKE LOG

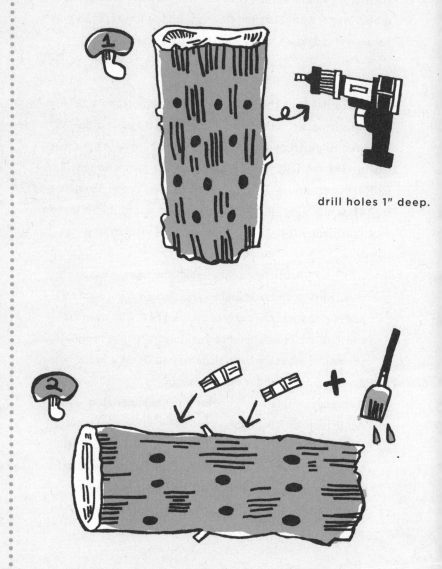

drill holes 1" deep.

insert spawns and seal with wax.

place log in
ventilated plastic bag.

keep watered and harvest blooms!

of the holes. Then seal the holes with hot wax to keep them sterilized during incubation.

STEP 3: Now for the patience. Put your shitake log into a plastic bag with airholes slit into the bag and tuck it into a kitchen closet. But don't forget it! What makes shitakes work indoors, as opposed to many other mushrooms, is that the log doesn't need to touch soil—but it does need to stay moist. The plastic bag should help retain moisture: Check it regularly and count on watering your log about once a week. (Just work it in with your weekly indoor watering.)

STEP 4: Once your shitakes start to bloom, you will have fresh mushrooms for 4–5 years from one log. The flushes will come at intervals, and soaking a log in ice water will help trigger them.

### USING DRIED MUSHROOMS

Fresh mushrooms are surprisingly versatile in the kitchen. Sautéed, they enhance just about any sauce, or throw them in an omelet. Don't forget about trying them raw either; tossed with vinaigrette they make a great salad. But if you have a real bumper crop you may want to try drying your mushrooms.

Strolling through a Chinatown, you'll see bags of sliced and dried shitakes. These mushrooms dry and reconstitute well, and drying intensifies their flavor. Dried mushrooms can be stored indefinitely and reconstituted by soaking. Even after soaking, the texture is never like fresh ones, but dried shitakes are perfect for adding to vegetable stock and soups.

You can dry mushrooms in the sun or in an oven, but if you invest in a home-use dehydrator, you have increased control and can use this for other fruits and vegetables as well. A top-of-the-line unit ranges from $50 to $100 and is advised if you live in a really humid place. To prepare, slice the mushrooms, set them on drying trays or racks, and sun-dry (protect from insects and flies) or put them in the oven (at 100–150 degrees F). Or put them into your dehydrator and follow the instructions. After they are dry, place them in airtight bags or jars and store.

To reconstitute the dried mushrooms, place them into a bowl with warm water and cover for 30–45 minutes or until they're soft and supple. You can also add ½ cup of red wine to the mix for richer mushrooms for cooking. The liquid you soaked them in will be flavored, so use this for cooking the dish or save it for stocks later.

# *Chapter* (2) HANGING GARDENS
## TERRACES AND BALCONIES

A woman I knew in Brooklyn kept pots of herbs on her windowsill. She told me they did just fine, except when the graffiti taggers passed through and the tender sprouts got splattered. Realtors in New York often confuse "balcony" with "fire escape." While it is illegal to garden on a fire escape, if the area is not used for egress and really is a small balcony, you can get creative and make good use of this space as the garden of your "cozy" apartment. One way to do this is to hang windowboxes and securely fasten pots on the balcony rails; the other is to find hooks or other secure fastenings already mounted on the building or windowpanes that you can hang baskets from.

My friend Stacy grows produce on her tiny balcony in West Hollywood; her philosophy is, "the tougher a city is to live in, the more resilient and adaptable the unwanted visitors are." She's talking about raccoons and squirrels, and to thwart their efforts to gain access, she uses old security system hinges that still jut out over her windows. Here she hangs upside-down vegetable growers with tomatoes and cucumbers. She called me from the farmer's market for advice on which heirloom tomato to get, and I suggested '100 Cherry'. These are prolific, and sweet, and they resist many diseases. If you can go more specialty, try 'Sweet Baby Girl'. Remember the old adage: "A plant only grows as big as its pot." A tomato plant that can grow to 5 feet in a yard might only grow to 1 foot in a container because its roots are restricted. Stacy also wanted advice on cucumbers, but the farmer's market wasn't selling Baby Persian 'Green Fingers' cucumbers, which are great for growing in containers and ready to eat at 3–5 inches long. Instead, she found lemon cucumbers, which are also great for small containers and are my favorite for making gazpacho.

Stacy thinks she has outsmarted the raccoons and squirrels, but my money is on the rodents. Though I did hear a tip recently from a woman who filled an Oreo cookie with a jalapeño pepper and set it out for the raccoons. They ate it and never, ever came back. So along with your other edibles, plant spicy peppers to discourage grazing.

cherry tomatoes

cilantro

shallots

'serrano' peppers

## Pico de Gallo Balcony

### 'VICTORIA MEXICAN' HEIRLOOM TOMATOES

You will be lucky to find these cherry tomatoes as starts at your local nursery, but their flavor and beauty make them worth starting indoors at home. Make sure you harden off the plants for a few weeks before transplanting them outdoors. Then put them in a container or hanging basket, depending on the room you have available. Water about every other day, depending on your weather, and add fertilizer about every two weeks. If they are growing upright in a container, they may need to be staked.

### 'SERRANO' PEPPERS

*Serrano* means "from the mountains," and these hot peppers are wildly used in Mexico. They're about five times spicier than jalapeños, so they make for good raccoon deterrent. If you pick them when they are green, they are at their youngest and least spicy; the closer they come in color to red, the hotter they become. The plants only grow about 24–36 inches tall, so they are good for containers and small spaces. Even the peppers themselves are fairly small. Place the plants in full sun, and water and fertilize them as you would the tomatoes (see above).

### CILANTRO

If a section of your balcony gets more shade than sun, save it for your cilantro. It will start to go to seed once the temperature is consistently hot, so pinch back any flowers that form. (If they do flower, they will then form seeds—these are the herb coriander. Use the seeds for cooking, or save and replant them.)

Aphids don't like hot peppers, so grow a few extra. If you have aphids, put 2 whole 'Serrano' peppers and one peeled garlic clove into a blender with 2–4 cups of water. Blend well, and spray infested plants with the mixture. If you don't have fresh peppers, cayenne boiled with garlic will make an effective "anti-aphid" tea.

# Pico de Gallo Salsa

This is essentially an uncooked salsa, so you will want to season it to taste—that is, with more or less 'Serrano' pepper flavor.

* *12 'Victoria Mexican' cherry tomatoes*
* *1 small or medium shallot*
* *1–3 'Serrano' peppers (as many as you can take)*
* *¼ cup cilantro*
* *Pinch of salt*
* *Juice of 1 lime*

Dice the first four ingredients coarsely and add the salt and the lime juice. Mix it together and let it sit in the refrigerator for 2–3 hours for the flavors to meld. This is very good as dip with chips, and the freshness seems to go really well with fish tacos. It's best fresh, so plan on using the salsa within a day.

Cilantro likes morning sun and afternoon shade. Have some seeds on hand so you can start new plants throughout the season. Wait until each plant is 4–6 inches tall before harvesting; then cut off the outer leaves first.

### SHALLOTS

Since we are talking about very limited space here, I would grow shallots rather than onions. These cost more at the grocery store, and when used, especially raw, have a more mellow, refined flavor than many onions. The shallot is actually a bulb, so you will place these bulbs in your potting soil: The part with roots (or root scar) should be facing down. Cover with a thin layer of soil that just covers the bulb. Plant them in the fall for spring harvest, or in spring for late summer/autumn harvest. You know they are ready to harvest when their leaves yellow, wither, and droop over.

# Containers for Small Spaces

Even if your terrace or balcony is small, you can turn it into a favorite room of the house or apartment. I'm amazed at all the city dwellers who use their outdoor space for storage. If you install a garden, you've essentially added an addition to your home. And it's often the most relaxing place to enjoy a morning coffee or an evening glass of wine.

## GETTING STARTED

You want to find out how much weight your terrace can safely hold. Ask your co-op board, your landlord, or if the building is new, the engineer and architect who designed and built it. You don't want your containers to be so heavy as to stress the structural integrity of the building, but you also don't want your containers flying off your windy terrace because they don't weigh enough. A good rule of thumb is 30 pounds per square foot, including the containers, soil, and plants. In order to stay in this weight limit, look for planters other than ceramic and terra-cotta, such as resin and zinc. Keep in mind that the smaller the container, the more often a plant needs to be watered and the less space the plant has to grow. Oftentimes, a plant in a small container has a much more limited lifespan, so choose the largest pots you can, rather than several smaller ones.

Remember that containers really define the style of your outdoor space. I avoid the ubiquitous plastic ones. Many zinc containers do not cost that much more than plastic and look sleek and stylish. For bigger spaces, you can even consider using feed tanks from agricultural supply stores. For the volume they hold, they are very reasonable price wise and look nice. In addition, consider white cedar or teak containers, which weather well and generally fall into the appropriate weight range.

STEP 1: Choose lightweight but durable containers. The planter should be approximately 2–4 inches bigger than the root-ball of your plant.

STEP 2: Make sure each planter has drainage. Wood planters allow water to spill through the boards, but many zinc and resin planters will need to have holes drilled in the bottom of them.

make sure planter has drainage holes.

top with mulch.

add soil mix.

spread layer of fabric.

fill bottom with
lightweight rocks.

**STEP 3:** Place the planter on some sort of feet or lift. You can use plastic rings or ceramic pieces from gardening stores, or you can make funky lifts by screwing on lion's paws, antique doorknobs, or even billiard balls. Just make sure your container is not sitting flush on the surface, so the water has somewhere to drain.

**STEP 4:** Use a lightweight but organic drainage material at the bottom of the container. Volcanic rocks work well with edible plants. Fill about one-eighth of the container with these.

**STEP 5:** Layer landscaper or weed block fabric over your drainage material. Measure it out, cut it to size, and place it in the container. This helps keep soil from draining out during watering.

**STEP 6:** Mix organic potting soil with plenty of perlite for drainage. If the soil doesn't already contain worm castings, add those as well. Toss all the elements of your soil with a trowel.

**STEP 7:** Remove your plant from the nursery container. Either eyeball the soil level, or place the plant in the container to estimate the level. Remember that potting soil is not very dense; after watering, it will compact. Estimate a few inches higher than you think you will need, but not so much that the soil will be spilling over the rim of the container. The dirt surface should come to a few inches below the rim of the planter. Massage the roots so they become loosened and are not rootbound—that is, make sure the roots are not wrapped around themselves.

**STEP 8:** Check the soil level. If the level is appropriate, start adding potting soil around the root-ball until the level is a few inches from the container's rim. Press the soil down gently, and add more potting soil if needed.

**STEP 9:** Add 1–2 inches of mulch around the base of the plant to help retain moisture during the growing season and to add insulation in the winter. If you're in a very temperate climate, plant small, decorative plants around the edge so they cascade down the side of your container.

**STEP 10:** Water thoroughly, until water runs out of the bottom of the container.

# Fig Varieties

| FIG VARIETIES | BEST REGION | PREPARATION SUGGESTIONS |
|---|---|---|
| **Black Mission** Classic deep-purple skin with maroon center. | Well adapted to most regions, but needs to be wrapped in areas with cold winters (below freezing). | Anything from fig cake to pizza with fig and caramelized onion. |
| **Desert King** Green skin and sweet amber centers. | Coastal California, Pacific Northwest, Gulf Coast. | Raw with plain yogurt and walnuts, or dry them for snacks. |
| **Brown Turkey** Large, brown with amber center. | California, Southwest. | Stuff with goat cheese, wrap with prosciutto, and grill. |
| **Panachee** Yellow-green striped with raspberry jam-like center. | Hot climate areas with a long growing season. | Add to salad with mozzarella and mixed greens. |

## THE PERFECT FIG

Figs like growing in containers, and their big glossy leaves make them lovely ornamental trees in their own right. Once a little exotic in many parts of the country, fig trees are now appearing for sale in outlet stores, at farmer's markets, and even in some hardware stores. Figs are not a neutral fruit—not many people merely "like" figs. They either shy away from them or they love

# Fig Varieties

| FIG VARIETIES | BEST REGION | PREPARATION SUGGESTIONS |
|---|---|---|
| **Black Jack** Green-brown skin with red center. | Texas, Southeast. Small tree in a container for colder regions. | Great fresh, or preserve them in their own syrup. |
| **Violette de Bordeux** Small, deep-purple fruit with strawberry center and complex, lingering flavor. | Grows well in most regions. Suited to containers. | Eat raw, fresh, and immediately before raccoons get them. |
| **Hardy Chicago** Black-purplish skin with strawberry center. | Coastal Atlantic regions. Bred for colder climates. Good for containers. | Versatile—eat them fresh with pecans or make a chicken stuffing. |

them. The French writer Paul Valéry is quoted as stating, "You may deprive me of anything you like except coffee, cigarettes, and figs."

There's nothing as decadent as a box of fresh figs. Then there is fig paste, fig vinegar, fig ice cream, figs roasted in port and served over olive oil cake, fig and arugula salad, figs baked in focaccia, and fig and pork tacos!

Most people know the two most common figs—the 'Black Mission' fig and the 'White Katoda'. The Mission fig, named after the Mission of San Diego founded by Franciscans in 1769, was the first introduction of the dark-skinned, pink-fleshed figs to North America. Other varieties didn't start arriving until the 1850s. The Kadotas, with thick yellowish-green skin and super-sweet amber centers, were popular for canning in the 1920s.

Breeders are creating fig trees, such as 'Chicago Hardy', that withstand cold winters without being wrapped, and 'Petite Negra', that will even fruit indoors. In the Southeast, 'Celeste' is commonly grown, and in Texas, 'Magnolia' performs well.

The differences between a tree-ripened fig and a store-ready fig are profound. Visually, the store fig is unmarred and looks more appealing. Tree-ripened figs have seams cracking their flesh and are much juicier and more flavorful. Maybe you think you've been kissed before, but until you try a 'Panachee' or a sun-warmed 'Black Mission' fig right off the tree, you're a fig virgin as far as I'm concerned. Very few people have the luxury of tasting a fig at its best—this is why you want to grow your own fig tree. Wait until their skins are starting to crack (these imperfections indicate the peak of flavor) and don't hold or hoard

After serving oysters on the half shell, I wash the shells thoroughly and save them. I put the shells in a bag and beat them with a hammer, and when I am planting a new fig tree in a container, I add the crushed shells. They provide a slow release of lime and calcium that figs like.

them as they only last a day or two after picked. In his *Meditations* Marcus Arelius wrote about the cracked fig and beauty:

> *Figs, also, when they are quite ripe, begin to crack . . . so that if one has sympathy with the operations of the universe, and a profound insight into them, everything connected with them, even accidentally, will be seen to have a beauty of it own.*

### FIG TREE CARE

Place your fig tree in full sun. These are Mediterranean trees, so make sure you don't overwater or overfertilize them. I add a little bonemeal to the pots at the start of the growing season. Once your tree is established, prune the branches back in early spring after the last frost has passed.

Fig trees go dormant in the winter—they are not dead. Their roots can get damaged from the cold if they are in a pot. So if you live in a cold climate, try to bring your potted fig tree indoors for the winter. Even a garage or storage shed will work. Since the tree is dormant in winter, you'll only need to water it about once a month. If you have nowhere to store the tree indoors, you can take your chances leaving it outdoors, but wrap it with burlap for the winter.

## REMEMBER TO WATER!

Mysteriously, people's gardens tend to die when they are away on vacation in the summer's hottest, driest months. I encourage clients to have irrigation systems. I like to water my own garden, but since I have lots of figs to give away, friends and neighbors step in when I leave town. The reason I enjoy watering my garden myself is that I know when it rains and when it's especially hot and dry and I can adjust accordingly. I also like to see how everything is growing and to fuss over my plants a little. As well, I find it relaxing in a contemplative way. So if you have a small balcony or terrace with no outdoor spigot, you will most likely need to hand water. There's also the option of self-watering planters. These have a reserve in them, and after roots have established themselves, you can water less, usually about every three weeks.

## HANGING WINDOWBOXES

Oftentimes with terraces and balconies, space is of the essence. I try to anchor the corners of this space with the large containers: Along the sides, I hang windowboxes so they are oriented to the outside of the balcony. As well, if your balcony has two or three sides open, but the fourth is against the wall of your apartment, then attach a few small hanging baskets to the wall. Since mint is so aggressive, it's good to keep it planted by itself. It's also really hearty. Try a few baskets of mint mounted against your wall.

WALL-MOUNTED PLANTER

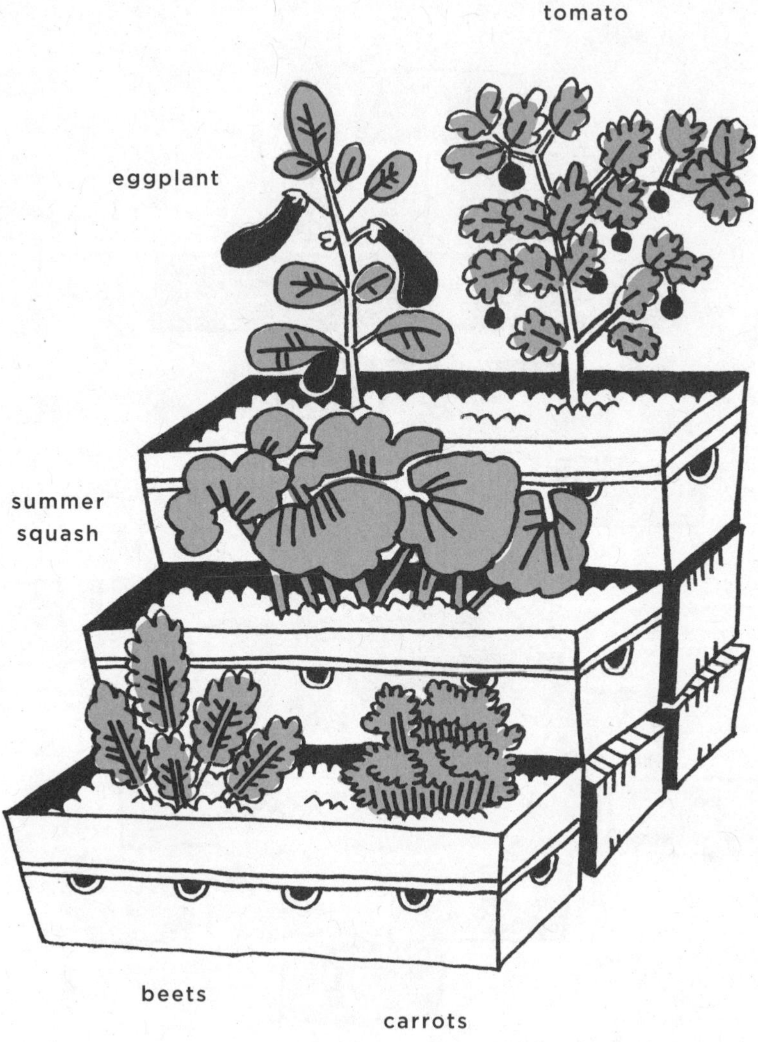

tomato

eggplant

summer
squash

beets

carrots

TERRACED PLANTERS

On the steep slopes of the Andes Mountains, the ancient Incans cut terraces to create more surface soil. They created retaining walls to hold the planting beds in place and dug irrigation canals with stone spouts to help curb erosion. In the carved-out mountains, they were the first in the world to cultivate potatoes. Other staples from Incan times included corn and quinoa.

Take a lesson from the Incas: Terracing is also a great space saver for small areas. You have a higher level in the back, then a lower level, or even three tiers. When using terraced planters, place your shorter plants in the front, so they aren't blocked and everything gets enough light. You can purchase three planters of the same size, abut them next to each other, and then use bricks (or other easily found recycled building materials) to create risers of staggered heights. This way, no plants are blocking each other from the sun, and they aren't casting shade on one another as they would be if lined up next to each other at the same level. Face them toward the south, if possible. The lower levels can benefit from reflected light. See the Resources Section on page 211 for where to purchase these already fabricated.

VERTICAL PLANTER

I'm still astonished that vertical planters work—living plants hanging on a wall. These can be as small as a picture frame or as big as an entire building. These are not gravity-defying plants, as it seems. Rather, rows of small planters have been inserted into a frame. These are angled downward so that the soil and plants don't tumble out. I would avoid the heavier plants, such as squash, melons, and even tomatoes. Instead, use this space for salad greens and herbs.

## Fruit Trees for Containers

Ultra-dwarf fruit trees are the smallest of the fruit trees, reaching 6–10 feet high. In containers and with pruning, they will stay even smaller and still produce lots of fruit, making them great for small terraces. These varieties of fruit trees are usually available as ultra-dwarfs: apple, pear, Asian pear, cherry, plum, apricot, nectarine, and peach.

Even better is the multivariety ultra-dwarf. Some fruit trees are self-pollinating, but many require a second species for cross-pollinating. One way to economize on space is to choose a tree that has several varieties grafted onto it. I have a very small cherry tree grafted with five different types of cherries. Some fruit appears earlier than others, so by having multiple grafts, you also get a longer fruiting season.

Growing on my rooftop, my ultra-dwarf, multigrafted cherry tree includes 'Stella', 'Rainer', 'Lambert', 'Montmorency', and 'Bing' cherries. The 'Stella' cherry fruit is dark red, almost black and very sweet. The 'Stella' variety is both self-fertile and a natural pollinator, so if you only get one tree,

If you have lots of cherries, you want to invest in a handy cherry pitter. I had to be persuaded by a friend to buy one, but now instead of letting surplus cherries sit in a bowl too long, I pit them and either freeze them in a heavy-duty plastic bag or cook them with some sugar or honey and water and seal them in a clean canning jar with anise stars. Then when the season has passed and I realize how much I had taken fresh cherries for granted, I take out the frozen ones or open a jar, remove the anise stars, and either eat the cherries mixed with Greek yogurt or make ice cream out of the anise cherries and shaved dark chocolate.

choose 'Stella'. But since it cross-fertilizes the others, it's great as part of a multigrafted tree.

I love sour cherries for jams, pies, and other pastries, and the 'Montmorency' cherries are great for these uses. The sour cherries come in late and have yellow, tart flesh. 'Rainier' you often see in grocery stores about mid-cherry season; it has yellow-red skin and is a crowd-pleaser. Then there's the 'Bing' cherry! This popular variety needs a pollinator, so for small areas it works best on a multigrafted tree. Cherry trees have the added benefit of beautiful spring blossoms.

### THE UBER-ULTRA DWARF

You can grow not just multiple varieties, but entirely different fruits on one tree. Some nurseries refer to these as "Tutti-Frutti" or "Fruit Salad." I like to call them the "uber-ultra." Usually you will find peach, nectarine, apricot, and sometimes

UBER-ULTRA DWARF
FRUIT TREE

plum all grafted onto one tree. Plant this small, productive tree in your sunniest corner and it will become a point of conversation; in fact, you might become known at work as the person with the "uber-ultra." If you really want to dazzle guests at your dinner party, pick some of your ripe stone fruits, halve and pit them, and sprinkle with sugar. Then broil them and serve hot over vanilla ice cream.

In very early spring and mid-fall, many fruit trees are available as bare-root specimens. They don't have leaves because they're in dormancy, and their roots are "bare" (that is, packaged without soil or container). Bare-root plants are much less expensive than the "balled and burlapped" ones you buy later in the season. Follow the directions for planting found on page 45–47. Also make sure that the graft or bud union, which often looks like a knob, is two inches above the soil. (This is where the trunk and the root system meet.) Then water deeply, but only water when the plant feels dry, which is less often than when the plant has leaves.

It seems counterintuitive that loping off branches is actually good for your tree, but it is. Pruning will help your tree stay healthy and provide larger and more colorful fruit. Prune every year in early spring, preferably before the flowers bloom.

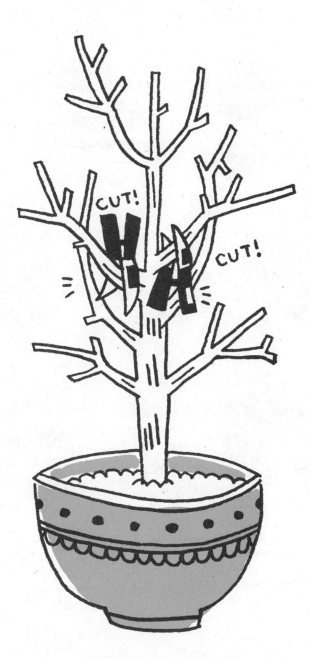

prune crowded or crossing branches
when plant is dormant.

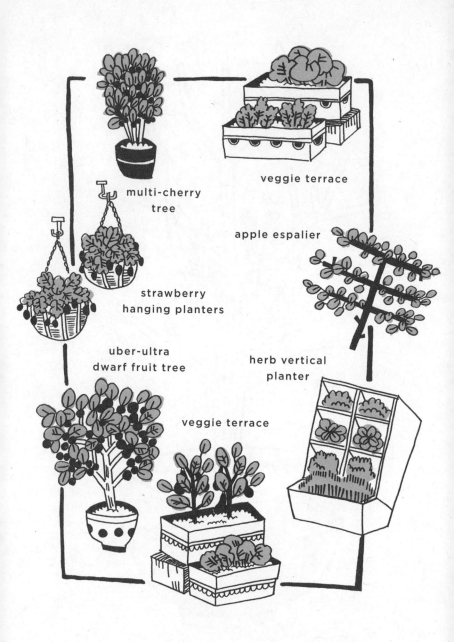

multi-cherry
tree

veggie terrace

apple espalier

strawberry
hanging planters

uber-ultra
dwarf fruit tree

herb vertical
planter

veggie terrace

SPACE-SAVING BALCONY

# Espaliers

I love espaliers. These are trees that have been pruned, shaped, and trained into two-dimensional works of art that decorate walls and can produce far more fruit than freestanding trees. Espaliers were painted on Egyptian tombs as early as 1400 B.C. In the Middle Ages, fruit trees were trained around a castle wall; this left open space in the grounds, and the branches decorated the bare walls. Sunlight reaches more parts of the branches, so the tree is more productive. As well, if you train it against a white or light-colored wall, it can benefit from reflected heat and light. By the seventeenth century in France, from Louis XIV's palace of Versailles to fencing around peasants' homes, espaliered trees could be found.

Since there was so much open space in the United States, espaliers really didn't catch on here for a while, but due to more small-space gardeners, they are becoming more popular, as espaliers are both beautiful and bountiful. The most popular are pears and apples. When choosing, look at their styles and varieties. Both pears and apples often require another variety for cross-pollination, so you can get multiple varieties of up to four different pear or apple types grafted on one three-tiered espalier, and some with as many as six on one with six arms (three tiers). In California, for example, I have seen 'Golden Delicious', 'Fuji', 'Gala', 'Red Delicious', 'Sraeburn', and 'Gravenstein' on one espalier! And at my local nursery, Green Jeans, they get in pear espaliers with 'Bartlett', 'Red Anjou', 'Comice', 'Bosc', 'Forelle', and 'Seckel'.

An espalier needs to be planted against a wall. Since the terrace espalier is in a container, it will already be 4–6 inches away from the wall. Either have a fixed trellis mounted on the

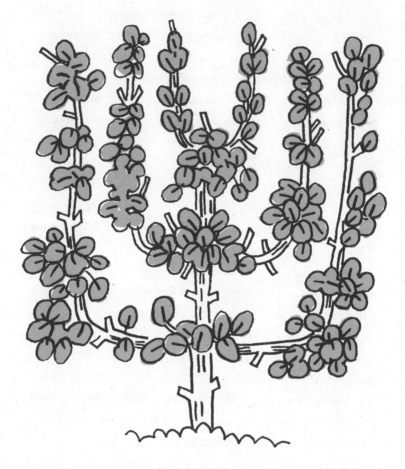

palmette verrier

ESPALIER TREE STYLES

informal

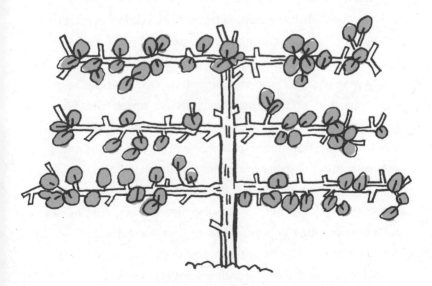

triple cordon

> Don't pick your apples too early! Lift an apple and twist it slightly; those that are ready should separate easily from the branch.

wall, or screw eyebolts into the wall, one at the end of each arm of the espalier. Pass wire through these and attach it firmly to the eyebolts. Use plant ties, twist ties, or bamboo shoots to fasten your espalier to the wire. This is the trellis it will grow on. The ties may need to be removed as the stem thickens, so avoid using wire fasteners, and check them a few times a year in order to loosen and prevent growth constriction.

### PRUNING

The arrival of the espalier to the United States is often credited to Henry Leuthardt. He learned this skill as a child in Switzerland, and after immigrating in 1922, he started a nursery on Long Island. According to Henry Leuthardt Nurseries, you might have to prune your espalier twice a year to help it keep its shape and enhance its productivity. Apple and pear espaliers bear fruit primarily on their spurs. These little upshoots come from the main branches. Don't prune the main branches until they reach the height and length that you want.

If you prune during the dormant season or before the plants flower, it will help to stimulate new growth. Pruning in midsummer (June or July) tends to have a dwarfing effect. Avoid pruning in late summer, except to cull off small shoots. Branches not needed for the design should be removed.

# The Native Wildlife Terrace

Originally from Montana, my friend Schjanna is a fashion designer. When she bought her co-op in Clinton Hill, Brooklyn, we knew her tiny terrace garden needed to be like her—chic and a little wild. We decided to create an all-native garden and register it as an official wildlife habitat with the National Wildlife Federation. Her interior was decorated in white and silver, so we custom built containers out of lightweight wood. Rather than fill them with soil, we made a way to drop shallow, inexpensive planters into them. We then covered the planters with a facade of weather-proofed pressed aluminum that looked like vintage tin.

There are four main elements for wildlife habitat: food, shelter, water, and sustainability. We also wanted "edibility" in the garden. We purchased native plants that provided food for birds, bees, and butterflies. These included black-eyed Susans, purple coneflowers, bee balm, and coreopsis. As for native edibles, we added two small serviceberry trees that have beautiful white flowers in early spring and edible berries in late summer. They need to cross-pollinate, so we installed two

You don't want pears to ripen on the trees, but you also don't want them too young or hard. Feel for a little "give" in the flesh, and then if it's there, the fruit should twist easily from the tree. If you put pears in brown paper bags, they will ripen in a few days. 'Anjou' and 'Bosc' require at least 30 days of refrigeration after they are picked.

in blossom

with fruits

ELDERBERRY

of them. We put in a box of clumping native raspberries, but didn't mix them with the others as they root on runners and will spread aggressively. Then we mixed four small blueberry plants in with the native flowers. These have modest cream blooms in the spring and great fall interest as their leaves turn russet and burgundy.

We also added two elderberry shrubs. When the flamboyant poet Oscar Wilde visited the United States, he declared that he wanted to meet Walt Whitman, a more homespun and modest bard. Wilde was quoted as saying, "I come as a poet to call upon a poet." After Wilde told Whitman that his mother had read *Leaves of Grass* to him as a child, Walt Whitman declared, "I will call you Oscar," and he pulled out a bottle of elderberry wine and the two drank it. Elderberry is perfect for Europe meets North America. Both Native Americans and ancient Greeks made flutes from the stalks; it has been used medicinally, ingested, as it has lots of antioxidants and vitamin C. It has been used as a skin tonic to soothe burns and as a tonic. And it's appropriate that a poet like Whitman, who waxes rhapsodic about nature, should appreciate this plant. Its flowers attract hummingbirds, bees, and butterflies. As well, the berries are delicious made into tempura.

Elderberry attracts the good bugs like lacewings. Female lacewings lay about 300 eggs, and each developing larvae eats between 1,000 and 10,000 aphids. Aphids are one of the worst things that can happen to an edible garden.

For the water element, we designed and created a fountain out of aluminum, which operates on a solar pump. It had one level that was very shallow for beneficial insects and another deeper level for the birds.

We discussed building a kestrel box, but then realized that making a garden to attract wildlife—and then adding a predator—would not make for a peaceful, relaxing environment. So we decided on a bat box instead. The exterior was painted black so it would absorb more sun and help the bats stay warm. We then mounted it in a sunny spot on the terrace. Schjanna's boyfriend was doubtful about the bat box until she explained that a bat eats up to 600 mosquitoes a night.

As for sustainability, we mulched with marble chips for a clean, modern look, as well as to retain moisture and keep the weeds down. Then Schjanna bought a tiny kitchen compost bin. She takes her organic waste to the local famer's market and in exchange gets fertile compost to add to her container garden.

## The Spa Terrace

A woman in my dance class asked me for tips about her small terrace—she wanted a space to relax and to do yoga. That's when the idea of a small spa terrace occurred to me. She could have chaise lounges in the center that could be folded and moved so that she could unfurl her yoga mat. Surrounding these, I suggested that she plant the flowers, fruits, and vegetables that spas traditionally use in treatments.

Herbs have long been cultivated for their culinary and medicinal uses, while their scents are prized in and of themselves as therapeutic. They have the power to transport, relax, or revitalize you. Many soaps, shampoos, candles, and body lotions are scented with them, so there is no reason why you can't grow and then create your own treatments. I'm picturing this terrace with modern, simple containers that are beige and white.

# Lemon Verbena Bath Salts

* *2 sprigs lemon verbena*
* *1 cup sea salt*

Chop the lemon verbena into small pieces and mix with the sea salt. Let it sit for 2 weeks. The longer the herbs sit, the more the salt absorbs them. Mix them into a warm bath.

# Sage and Rose Petal Salt Scrub

Sage is a stimulating herb, and rose petals are soothing. I like the idea of combining these in a salt scrub to keep in your shower and use before you start your day. Sort of a giddy-up-whoa!

* *3 stems sage (with leaves)*
* *3 cups coarse sea salt*
* *½ cup rose petals*
* *10 ounces jojoba or almond oil*

 Take the sage stems and dice them finely or put them in a food processor.

 Mix with the sea salt, and then fold in the rose petals.

 Pour jojoba or almond oil into the jar until the salt is entirely covered. Store this in your bathroom, and use it in the shower to exfoliate.

Lemon verbena is really easy to grow. It likes sun and for its soil to be on the dry side. This plant should come indoors for the winter (it will lose its leaves and then regenerate them the following summer). The leaves smell wonderful and retain their scent for quite some time when dried, so they are a good bet for making bath salts.

## APRICOT TREES

Apricot trees are great to have for ornamental purposes, as they have lovely pink and white flowers in the springtime and then are laden with fruit in mid- to late summer. After this their leaves turn yellow and russet-red before the tree goes dormant for the winter.

They are also very versatile, as they handle temperatures from minus 30 to 100 degrees F. If you live somewhere that has long stretches of extreme heat or extreme cold, wheel them indoors during the hot or cold blasts. They are self-pollinating, so you only need one tree, which is practical on a small terrace.

Remember to keep your apricot tree watered and to add organic fertilizer or fruit tree food at least once a month. When the tree is dormant, prune it by removing any unhealthy branches or limbs that are intersecting or hampering others.

Apricots are rich in vitamin A, and so are often used topically for skin care. As well, they have vitamin C, and lots of amino acids and enzymes. Apricots make your hair stronger, more pliant, and shinier. But the best way to benefit from all the health benefits of apricots is to eat them.

# Apricot Face Mask

* *3 apricots*
* *2 tablespoons milk*
* *1 tablespoon honey*

1. Remove the pits of the apricots.

2. Purée the fruit, milk, and honey together.

3. Spread the mask over your face with upward strokes. Leave on for 10 minutes, then rinse with warm water.

# Apricot Smoothie

* *3 ripe apricots*
* *2 cups low-fat yogurt*
* *1 cup orange juice*
* *1 tablespoon wheat germ or flax seeds*

Put the apricots, yogurt, and orange juice into a blender or food processor. Liquefy, then sprinkle some wheat germ or flax seeds on top.

The best time to harvest leaves and flowers for tea is in the morning, just after the dew has dried but before the sun gets hot. Then rub or bruise the leaves to release the essential oils.

### VIOLETS

Plant patches of violets under a tree or shrub on your terrace. Harvest and dry both the leaves and flowers and steep them in tea. The fragrance is wonderful, and the tea is a good source of vitamins A and C.

### BERGAMOT

Also known as monarda or bee balm, this is an excellent plant to have in your terrace garden. Plant it in full sun and keep it watered. You want to harvest the leaves for tea before the flowers bloom. Bee balm tea helps relieve symptoms of colds, flu, and nausea. By mid- to late summer, the plant has big, bright bushy flowers that butterflies and hummingbirds love.

### CHAMOMILE

Chamomile can be used to fill in areas where you need a pretty little plant that is low growing and it makes for a nice ground cover. For tea, harvest the flowers when they are bright yellow. Once they turn dull, they are too old and have gone to seed. You can dry the seeds and plant them the following year.

rosehips

bergamot

chamomile

hibiscus

violets

HERBAL TEA POT

use just the calyx
for tea.

HIBISCUS

## HIBISCUS

There are many different species of hibiscus flowers, but the one most commonly made into tea is the hibiscus *sabdariffa*. These are for warmer climates, and don't like freezes. They bloom best when the temperature is between 60 and 90 degrees F. To harvest them, wait until the flower has bloomed and has fallen off; it's the calyx or outer bunch of leaves that you want. Wash them well and either dry them in the stove or out in the sun. Rich in vitamin C, hibiscus tea is also believed to aid in weight loss if a cup is consumed after meals as it helps reduce the absorption of carbohydrates.

# The Guy Terrace

A friend of mine in San Francisco works one of those thousand-hour-a-week tech jobs, but still wants to enjoy his terrace in the millisecond that he has to relax. I suspect that he and his roommate want to try and seduce women on their terrace. And like a guy walking a puppy, the ladies do like a guy with a garden. My sister tells the story of a man she knew who had a hibiscus plant he had named Windy (pronounced "Wendy"). Telling women about Windy—how he found her on the street, blown over and abandoned, took her home, and nursed her back to health—turned that hibiscus into a babe magnet. And though it seems to speak of a sensitive nature, my sister reported that the guy was a total player.

And just imagine a man who feeds you from a plant in his sexy terrace garden? Well, he's in with the ladies. Here's his plant list: really large Mission fig tree (I consider figs to be the oysters of the fruit world). The hardscape consists solely of one large, white planter. To give it more flair, I suggested purchasing one that is illuminated at night. There are some nice ones that come with lights already in them; other resin ones can be drilled and lights inserted. Then there's the make-out couch with modular seating, a deep-cushioned couch, white outdoor fabric, and dark wood or tightly woven dark mesh.

*Chapter* **3** **MOVING ON UP**
ROOFTOP GARDENS

*Chapter* **3** **MOVING ON UP**
ROOFTOP GARDENS

Sky-high oases are coveted for the view, the privacy, and the sense of being luckier than everyone else. I named my business Prospect & Refuge after a theory developed by geographer Jay Appleton. His prospect-refuge theory describes a space where we have the best view but don't feel exposed or unprotected. Think of a queen addressing the crowd from a balcony—it's strategic. This is why we don't like to sit with our backs to the door; we feel safe when looking at a view from a rocky cliff above a valley or standing on a rooftop terrace overlooking a city. Rooftop gardens that provide both retreat and perspective are examples of this philosophy. When designing a rooftop or balcony space according to the prospect-refuge theory, keep in mind that you want both the best view and an intimate space.

As well, no two rooftops are the same. Some have more wind and are exposed to scorching sun, and others are shaded; each one is its own little Galápagos Island, a small ecosystem that evolves in some natural and, at times, unnatural ways. Diversity of conditions is the fun and the challenge of rooftop gardens. When evaluating your rooftop space, first find your best view. Is there a river or lake to one side and a highway to the other? I once had a client point down from her terrace and say, "A co-worker lives there. I'd prefer it if she couldn't see me here." Consider plants that create a screen from nosey neighbors but still allow you to enjoy the rest of the view. If you're lucky enough to have part of your rooftop garden exposed to water, then that may mean you get lots of wind, particularly during the winter months. Evaluate your wind conditions. In this chapter, I've listed ideas for hearty edible plants that can tolerate high winds and protect other, more delicate plants.

Also check how much sunlight you get—rooftops can be very hot and dry. If this is the case, you might consider creating a Mediterranean-style edible garden (see page 88) with drought-tolerant plants that don't mind soaring temperatures, direct sunlight, and dry soil between waterings.

Often, because rooftops have full sun exposure, they can yield remarkable crops. In 1993, Dr. Job Ebenezer, director of Environmental Stewardship and Hunger Education at the Evangelical Lutheran Church in Chicago, led a movement to install an edible rooftop garden using children's wading pools for planters. By 1997, one pool alone produced about 22 pounds of vegetables. So for rooftop homesteaders, there's precedence. The following suggestions are for easy ways to create a beautiful rooftop space to relax and entertain, surrounded by specialty heirloom edibles mixed with colorful flowers. Add an opera table, bistro chairs, and a café umbrella, and you will feel like you've escaped to France whenever you sit in your garden.

## The Windy Rooftop

There's no reason you can't have an edible garden on a windy rooftop. Most vegetables are annuals that grow during spring and summer, which tend to be the mildest seasons. So you can hope for the best or try to put hearty plants between tender ones for protection. For your fruit trees and shrubs, select them carefully. Some plants are more delicate than others and can dry out quickly; others may have a problem with their leaves shedding or can be denuded of their blossoms, killing any chance of fruit. One way to remedy these problems is to grow plants naturally found on beaches that adapt well to windswept areas.

In order to create both privacy and to respect a view, try to "anchor" your rooftop's corners. Use groupings of three containers that match in style, yet vary slightly in size. You want to choose these plants not just for their ability to handle windy conditions, but also for their shape, color, texture, bloom time, and year-round interest. They may also create a protective screen for more delicate plants. Between these containers place rectangular planter boxes filled with shrubs and low-growing plants.

### SEA BUCKTHORN

In Russia where the sea buckthorn thrives, it has been referred to as the "Siberian pineapple." Since it adapted well to the place poets and rebels were sent to perish under Soviet-era dictators, it can stand up to harsh conditions, such as the Chicago-style winds coming off of the Great Lakes. For gardens on the windswept Long Island Sound or near the tempestuous Pacific Ocean, sea buckthorn also tolerates salinity from the saltwater that storms through.

The plant has beautiful silver-green leaves and clusters of orange fruit that wrap around its dark branches. The berries add color well into autumn. Although the fruit is bitter (I'll hold back Soviet Gulag comments here), juice from the berries is often mixed into sweeter juices because it contains vitamins C, A, and E. It's thought that sea buckthorn may have been the first fruit juice consumed in space, by Soviet cosmonauts. Technically, the Tang that American astronauts drank is not a juice.

### PINEAPPLE GUAVA

The pineapple guava, which has a light-green leaf with the texture of suede, withstands wind and extreme temperatures, salt spray, and drought. To boot, it has showy white flowers with bright-red stamens. The petals have a fragrant, sweet taste and are nice tossed in salads or as a garnish for desserts. Birds also love to eat them—but don't fret, birds eating the flowers is how they cross-pollinate. The blooms develop into a jammy fruit with a tropical flavor that tastes surprisingly like pineapple and guava. Plant more than one for pollination purposes and to help protect your terrace from the wind.

### BEACH PLUM

Excellent plants for windy conditions, beach plums have a profusion of beautiful white flowers in the springtime. They are native on the Atlantic Coast, but do well throughout the country. For a lower-lying hedge, select the variety 'Cotuit', which grows only to 2–3 feet high and produces lots of small (¼ inch–1 inch) sweet fruit. Wait until the plums are totally ripe before you eat them or they can be really sour.

### RUGOSA (BEACH) ROSE

Another favorite of mine are rugosa roses. These coastal beauties have peak summer blooms of white or magenta with bright gold centers. Their rosehips are also lovely and create autumn interest. Pluck these and make rosehip jelly, or string and hang them to dry so you can brew them as a vitamin C–rich herbal tea to ward off colds in the winter.

### LAVENDER

Throughout your boxes of beach plums and beach roses, plant clumps of lavender. The silvery gray foliage adds a nice texture, and you can use the blossoms for everything from herbal bath salts to mixing with egg whites when making a lavender–lemon meringue pie. As well, the plants attract hummingbirds.

### MAYPOP/PASSION FRUIT

A surprisingly hearty edible is the passion fruit. I love when the word *rampant* is used to describe a plant, and it is often applied to this beauty. When Christian missionaries arrived in the Americas and saw the profusions of beautiful flowers spreading on vines, they used the petals to teach the natives about the apostles, illustrated the crown of thorns with the tendrils, and represented the Holy Trinity with the stamens. So while many people might think the bloom was named passionflower for its seductive stamen, come-hither purple color or delicate petals, it's not; it's named for the Passion of Christ.

I always assumed the taste of Hawaiian Punch was from a delicate balance of processed sugar and red dye #2, but it is said that it actually comes from passion fruit. One tropical species of passionflower is most commonly purple or yellow. These are seed-filled fruits in a gelatinous pulp that is sour and delicious. If you live in a place where temperatures drop below freezing, consider this plant an annual or grow it in a pot that you bring indoors for the winter. The 'Black Knight' *passiflora* is a purple variety developed specifically for pots by Patrick Worley in Massachusetts. Its fruit is touted as being fragrant, dark purple-black, and the size and shape of a large egg.

As well, there's the 'Maypop' passionflower that is indigenous to the southeastern part of the United States and grows wild in the Midwest. It has a yellow fruit the shape of a chicken egg and a delicious seedy/pulpy center.

## Screening and Underplanting

If you have your heart set on a tender dwarf apricot or chocolate persimmon tree, create a screen with hearty evergreens and ornamental grasses to protect your dwarf fruit trees from the winds without blocking their exposure to the sun. If you block southern sunlight with your windbreak, plant shade-tolerant blueberries, and around the base of shrubs, grow spinach. In chapter 4, there is more information on planting an edible forest (see page 135), but underplanting is a similar idea, just on a smaller, simpler scale.

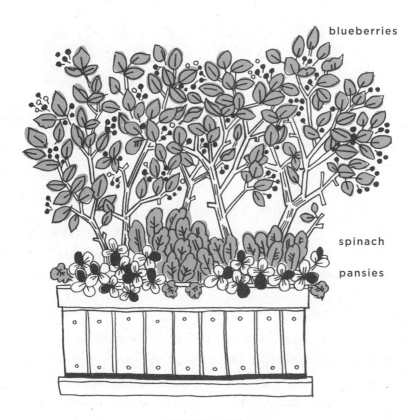

blueberries

spinach

pansies

UNDERPLANTING

### BLUEBERRIES

Blueberries like acidic soil, so to prepare pots, mix equal parts of peat moss and potting soil together. Also, you can purchase organic fertilizers that are acid heavy, such as seaweed mixtures, to add when watering. Highbush blueberries can grow as tall as 6 feet, but certainly won't in a container. Midsize bushes grow to about 2 feet, and the lowbush blueberries are like a ground cover. For rooftop containers I'd recommend midsize varieties with early to late summer fruiting. The more different varieties you grow, the better the cross-pollination and fruiting. You'll have a longer blueberry season.

I've planted spinach and pansies under my blueberries, and they are very happy there. As well, leafy green vegetables help the soil retain moisture and so are good for the blueberries. Pansies are edible, but I mostly grow them as ornamentals.

## Cold Frame

On my windy, foggy, sunny, salty, rainy rooftop, only the most vigorous plants survive. So to nurse along my peppers and other delicate, heat-loving plants, I use a version of a cold frame. It is basically a small greenhouse that you can build or purchase (see page 207). It is ideal to have one built at an angle that can face the south; it should also have a lid that can be propped up an inch or two so that it vents easily when it gets hot outside. This way your plants are warm when it's cold but don't cook when it's warm and sunny. Basically, a cold frame is a box with a clear top and hinges so that it can be opened for airflow and so you can access the plants.

I made a very simple greenhouse out of an old teak table base and Plexiglas. You can also put old windows to use. A cold frame not only helps on a windy rooftop but also anywhere where you need a little more warmth and protection to get seedlings started.

BUILDING A COLD FRAME

# The Mediterranean Lounge Garden

The Mediterranean rooftop works best in dry climates, but people in many places can substitute a plant here and there. It's also possible to bring in a few of the planters for the winter and still enjoy the serene sophistication of a Mediterranean-style garden adapted to small spaces. In her book *Italian Villas and Their Gardens,* Edith Wharton wrote: "The traveler returning from Italy, with his eyes and imagination full of the ineffable Italian garden-magic, knows vaguely that the enchantment exists; that he has been under its spell..." On Sunday afternoons, your book club will love coming over to discuss Wharton's work set in Italy while surrounded by Mediterranean edibles like grapevines, olive trees, figs, pomegranates, lemon trees, lavender, and rosemary. When I host a book club meeting, I like to serve dishes that feature my rooftop garden—olives warmed with lemon, rosemary, and garlic; fig bread with a tangy cheese; raw oysters (use the shells later as fertilizer); a tossed salad with fresh pomegranate seeds; lemon meringue pie with lavender; and, of course, wine. As everyone knows by now, book clubs are not entirely about the books.

## A GRAPEVINE PRIVACY WALL

To create a sense of privacy and block an unsightly view, start with a trellis or privacy wall filled in with grapevines. Grapes grow quickly, have large, lovely leaves you can use to make dolmatis, and provide bountiful fruit in the autumn. Later, as winter approaches, the foliage turns a deep scarlet.

Grapevines are good for growing on rooftops as they like full sun. The more stressed they become from drought or winds, the more interesting their flavor will be. Stress causes

White roses are often planted in abundance in vineyards; you will often see them at the end of rows and clustered around walking paths. This is not just for their sheer beauty. Light-colored roses help grape growers determine if damp or foggy weather will threaten their crops. Roses are the canaries in the coal mine, so to speak, as signs of fungus will show up on their blossoms and foliage early and give growers time to dust their vines. Even though these have a pragmatic function, they create a subtle beauty in a Mediterranean garden.

them to put more energy into the fruit—living organisms have the instinct to reproduce when their lives are threatened. This is where winemakers tease the flavors of citrus and floral notes, chocolate undertones, or pepper from the grapes. If the plants are too stressed, they will die, so be careful. Most importantly, you need the right grape for the environment. Consult the grape cultivars chart on pages 93–94 for a list of popular varieties that can be grown in your region.

Grapevines can be installed to create a stunning privacy screen. Make just one of the planters to help create an intimate space, or use a series of them for a beautiful wall.

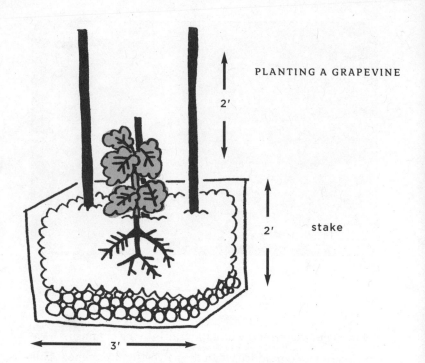

PLANTING A GRAPEVINE

2'

2'

stake

3'

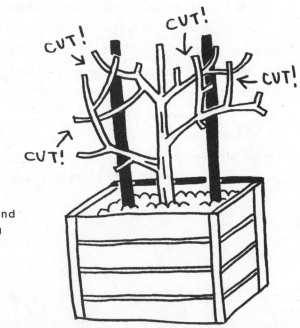

CUT!

CUT!

CUT!

CUT!

prune
crowded and
crossing
shoots.

**STEP 1:** Start with an outdoor planter that is made of hardwood, such as cedar or redwood, and is approximately 3 feet wide by 2 feet high. Fasten two wooden posts up either side. These should rise approximately 2 feet above the box. Measure 1 foot, and fasten an eye screw on either side. Run a heavy wire between these. At 2 feet, attach another one and run wire between them. You will also want a stake in the center of the box to support the grapevine.

**STEP 2:** Make sure your soil has plenty of drainage material. Purchase grapes that are 1–2 years old, in early spring. Bury them in the soil, leaving only a few inches of the tip visible. While they are young, keep the soil moist so the grapes don't desiccate.

**STEP 3:** As your grapevine grows, train it onto the first wire, spreading in both directions. As new tendrils sprout from the vine, they should reach up to the second wire. This method will help the branches receive more sun, and the plant will have fewer problems with mildew and fungus.

GRAPEVINE PRIVACY WALL

Grapes should be pruned during the dormant season. Very early spring, February, or March is when many vineyards prune. The older wood will have a thicker and darker bark (you usually don't prune this), and many new shoots will be sprouting from your cordoned branches. Go through and cut off about every third shoot, particularly the ones that seem to be jutting forward or backward. Try to keep the ones that are creating the shape you want. When there's new growth in the springtime,

To make raisins, you will need a few weeks of hot, dry weather. Pick the grapes and wash them well. Remove the stems, and spread the grapes over a screen or other drying rack. After a week, turn them. When they are dry, pack them in jars or plastic bags.

# Grape Varieties

| GRAPE VARIETY | BEST REGION | PREPARATION SUGGESTIONS |
|---|---|---|
| **Chambourcin**<br>Deep-purple grapes, hearty vigorous vine. | Originally from the cool coastal region of the Loire Valley in France. Fungus resistant and likes mild winters. Popular in the Pacific Northwest but also widely planted in the Midwest. | Deep-purple grapes make a nice snack fresh; can be fermented into a spicy wine; the large vigorous leaves are good for rolling dolmatis. |
| **Valiant**<br>This red grape can survive winters down to -70 degrees F. Produces fruit in a short growing season. | Michigan, Wisconsin, the Dakotas, Canada... it's the Viking grape. | Can be made into red wine, but has a sweet, tangy flavor so is great fresh. The taste is somewhat similar to a 'Concord' grape and is mostly used in jams and juices. Add cinnamon, cloves, and lemon peel to make a spiced jam to stash away for winter. |
| **Muscadine**<br>Native to Southeast. Likes warm and humid climates. In the wild, will grow 60–100 feet high. Has tough skin, but sweet, musky flesh. Variety 'Black Beauty' is popular. | Grows wild along the Atlantic seaboard from Florida to New York. Its territory is stretching west into Missouri and Texas. | Cook the juice with simple sugar syrup and make into sorbet, or add some tapioca to your juice and sugar and make a glaze for tarts. |

# Grape Varieties

| GRAPE VARIETY | BEST REGION | PREPARATION SUGGESTIONS |
| --- | --- | --- |
| **Concord** Grape juice, grape jam—with the unmistakable flavor of the blue-black grape. | Cultivated from the Pacific Northwest to the Eastern seaboard. | Eat as table grapes; make jellies, jams, and juices. |
| **Cayuga** Popular grape in the eastern United States. Hybrid French-American grape developed by Cornell. Very productive and disease resistant. | Upstate New York, Tri-State region, New England. | This grape is considered very versatile for wine-making. Has a floral quality and can be similar to a semidry Riesling or, if oak-aged, can have chardonnay characteristics. Freeze them whole and eat them as snacks or a light dessert. |
| **Muscat** Vines bloom with pale golden-yellow fruit. Found nationwide. | Likes heat, and can be grown in Oregon, coastal California, northern New Mexico, Missouri, and New York. | Serve these beauties fresh or try your hand at making a tangy, citrusy wine. |

prune the weaker, thinner shoots and keep the strong ones. Flowers will burst out, and these eventually turn to fruit. Like many vines, the more tendrils and shoots you cut back on a grapevine, the more energy will get sent into producing fruit. If you prefer more unruly grapevines, then prune less.

## OLIVE TREES

Aristotle is often associated with philosophy, not gardening, but he wrote a treatise on the cultivation and care of the olive tree. This was not an idiosyncratic interest, as the olive tree was part of the religion, was central to the economy, and its oil was considered a curative and a staple. Throughout the Mediterranean and Middle East, it was used as sacred oil in ceremonies, to anoint athletes, and even to prepare the dead.

For olive oils, many people like the Tuscan varietals, the most popular being 'Leccino' and 'Frantoio'. As well as being favored for oils, they are valued as table olives due to their flavor and high oil content. However, for brining, larger olives are preferred; in this case, you might want to go with the Spanish varietal 'Manzanillo'. As well, the Spanish varietal 'Arbequina' is a smaller tree that does well in containers. It can also be used as an espalier (see pages 63–66) or as a privacy wall similar to the grapevine. Just plant them and train the branches in the direction you'd like them to grow.

For people who live in colder climates, during winter you can move your planters somewhere cool but protected, such as into a garage. Olive trees like temperatures that run 32 degrees F overnight to 75 degrees F during the day. Really warm places like Florida are not ideal, as the trees need a true winter for some dormant time.

OLIVE TREE

# Zesty Warm Olives

This is a delicious and easy nibble to serve as an appetizer for parties. Just have plenty of crusty Italian bread alongside, to sop up the flavorful oil. It's fun to use a mix of different colors and sizes of olives for variety. To pit or not is up to you. The olives can be prepared up to 3 days ahead and refrigerated; warm before serving.

* *1 small lemon*
* *1 small sprig of fresh rosemary*
* *¼ cup extra-virgin olive oil*
* *1 teaspoon crushed red pepper*
* *1 garlic clove, minced*
* *1 pound brined olives*

1. With a vegetable peeler, remove the zest from the lemon in large swaths, being careful to avoid the bitter white pith. Slice the zest into narrow strips.

2. Remove the rosemary needles from the stem, and discard the stem (or save for other use, see page 15).

3. In a medium saucepan, combine the oil with the lemon zest, rosemary needles, crushed pepper, and garlic. Cook over moderate heat until the garlic barely begins to brown, about 5 minutes.

4. Remove from the heat, stir in the olives, and let stand for about 20 minutes, for the flavors to marry, before serving.

Olive trees prefer a well-drained loamy soil, so mix in a little extra perlite when planting. Use a lightweight potting soil, but avoid ones with too much fertilizer mixed in. Don't over-fertilize! I tend to err on loving plants to death. That's why I'm so excited about my worm composter—you really can't over-fertilize with worm castings, and they are compounds that are already broken down (see pages 2–7). Try to use organic, broken-down manures or compost for fertilizer—maybe an inch layer when planting. You can also test your soil's pH to see if you should add lime.

Don't overwater, and water even less one month before harvest to ensure more concentrated flavors. The major pruning should come after the harvest; light pruning of damaged or denuded branches can be done throughout the spring and summer until the tree is fruiting. After the harvest, spray copper that has been approved for organic gardening on your olive trees to avoid winter diseases like peacock spot and leaf fungus.

As well, many people have fruiting olive trees in their yards, but never harvest them and are more than happy to have others pick the olives before they fall on the ground. Don Landis teaches olive workshops in northern California. As he makes his rounds through Sonoma and Marin counties repairing refrigerators, he keeps an eye out for fruiting olive trees along highways and in residential yards. When he spots one he likes, he knocks on the door and asks the residents if he can harvest their tree. They almost always grant approval, as the fruit gets messy when it falls.

Olives can be picked green, when younger, or when black. Their flavors will vary accordingly: The green ones will have a sharper, grassier flavor, and the black ones a richer, mellower flavor when brined (though not when raw—they are acidic and make you pucker). Always get them off the tree, not from the ground, so they are free of bruises. After harvesting them, start brining ASAP. Landis uses a salt brine technique he learned from his Uncle Jim rather than lye, which is often used with olives. Weeks later, he shows back up at the olive-tree owner's door with a jar of specialty olives.

### POMEGRANATE TREES

Pomegranates have recently hit the market as a "superfood," touted for their high level of antioxidants. You can grow them in a container on your sunny rooftop. The ruby-red seeds of pomegranates have long been symbols of death and rebirth in Egypt and of fertility in the Middle Ages. In Greek mythology, the pomegranate is associated with Persephone and the renewal of the earth at springtime. In the D. H. Lawrence poem "Pomegranate," the fruit seems to represent a soul divided or women troubles:

> In Syracuse, rock left bare by the viciousness of Greek women,
> No doubt you have forgotten the pomegranate trees in flower,
> Oh so red, and such a lot of them.

The showy flowers of these trees—ranging from deep orange to bright red—are prized in and of themselves, and the round light-pink to dark-burgundy fruits are as ornamental as they are delicious.

The pomegranate is from Persia and grows well in arid places with long, hot summers, but it can tolerate freezing temperatures down to about 12 degrees F. If you live in a temperate

> Plant your lemon tree in a container slightly larger than what you think you may need. Around the base, plant cascading rosemary or small clumps of lavender. Terra-cotta might be too heavy for a rooftop (and real terra-cotta from Italy costs a fortune), so search for some earth-toned pots made of resin.

climate, a rooftop might create a more desertlike atmosphere. Place the tree somewhere with full sun or against a white wall, with reflected heat. It can be brought indoors for the winter.

Russian botanist Gregory Levin spent his life collecting and cultivating over a thousand types of pomegranates in the former Soviet Union state of Turkmenistan. When the Soviet Union collapsed and he lost state support, Levin smuggled a number of species to the University of Davis repository, where the scientist continues to grow many types of pomegranates. The early ripening ones tend to be sweeter and are a better bet if the climate is a little cooler. The pomegranate 'Sweet' is a small tree that is suited to pots and cooler summers. Other sweet varieties include 'Ambrosia' and 'Sin Pepe/Pink Ice', as well as the more obscure 'Myatadzhy', and 'Sirinevyi'. The sweet and tart varieties have a more complex and sought after flavor. These include 'Sharp Velvet', 'Medovyi Vahsha', and 'Palermo'.

### LEMON TREES

Meyer lemons, with their tempered tartness and lower acidity, are popular (see page 25), but some people prefer the bite of a true lemon. 'Eureka' and 'Lisbon' lemons are the most com-

prune branches at the trunk near bottom.

LEMON TOPIARY TREE

plant cascading rosemary at base.

monly found of these "true" lemons, but some of the more prized Mediterranean lemons include 'Genoa Lemon', which has a sharp, distinct flavor and beautiful foliage.

Mediterranean gardens often have rows of lemon trees shaped into topiaries that resemble a single ball. These are planted in terra-cotta pots and placed throughout patios and walkways. To shape your lemon tree into a single ball, start with a small tree and prune new growth from around the base or bottom of the tree. Let the top part of the tree grow naturally for a less neurotic look and so it can bloom and fruit.

## French Market Garden

Whether you love 'em or not, the French know food—including how to grow exquisite varieties in the most practical and beautiful way possible. You can plant containers that combine French intensive methods as well as potager garden planting techniques for a lovely and productive rooftop garden.

The age-old method of French intensive gardening essentially means tilling the soil deeply so roots don't have to work hard to find moisture or nutrients; the soil is fed with large amounts of compost and manure to keep it fertile. As well, crops are planted closely together to help crowd out weeds, and new seeds are started between the narrow rows so that when one crop is finished, a new one is ready to take its place.

A French kitchen potager garden is essentially an interplanting of vegetables, herbs, and flowers that all work together to increase flavor, enhance the soil, and attract beneficial insects. Plant special varieties and harvest when they are small—young green beans, known as haricots verts, radishes, carrots, and beets are rich with flavor and nutrients. You may have time to plant a second round of them.

Combining these two approaches—French intensive and potager—into a rooftop container garden makes perfect sense. I call this a French market garden, because when I first wandered through a French farmer's market, the fruits, vegetables, and flowers were riots of color and scents that infused the air with a sense of bounty and well-being. As well, the selections were much smaller than I was used to seeing, and I learned that this young, compact produce was more flavorful than the larger ones.

Start your garden with rich potting soil that has lots of organic compost. The larger the containers, the less you will need to water and the more varieties you can interplant. An ideal size would be that of an oak wine barrel cut in half. You can also use silver aluminum stock tanks that have a modern look to them, and these will help minimize your bending and kneeling.

The following sections suggest plants that are beneficial to each other. And while French intensive methods involve tilling deeply, if you use good potting soil, you can save yourself this labor and just toss it with a trowel. The aromatic herbs; bright, cheery flowers; and colorful, flavorful vegetables will make you want to lounge in your bistro chairs munching on miniature heirloom produce while reading French writer Colette wax rhapsodic about her garden:

> I have experienced the anguish and joy of perceiving life in the plant kingdom, not at the movies but through my feeble though complete senses, each shored up by the other, not by overloading or wildly exaggerating what my eyes see . . . between bud and bloom there takes place a miracle of effort, then of efflorescence.

The 'Precoce d'Argenteuil' asparagus turns white when blanched; the French heirloom variety has tips with a purple tint. Unlike many other asparagus varieties, which do not offer a decent harvest until the third year, 'Argenteuil' will give a good yield in the second year.

Chervil is in the parsley family, but the taste has a hint of licorice to it. This pungent herb helps keep aphids away and is lovely tossed fresh in a salad. Asters are daisylike lavender flowers. Native to North America, from Texas to North Dakota and New York to Colorado, they tend to do well in almost all places that have a sunny summer. Almost all flowers in the aster family, including sunflowers, marigolds, yarrow, and asylum, attract ladybugs, lacewings, and other beneficial insects that eat aphids and other damaging bugs. Use the produce of this planter to make a fabulous omelette Argenteuil (an omelet filled with sautéed asparagus tips).

## TROIS SOEURS

The haricot vert is a very thin, young green bean that is often used in recipes that call for blanched green beans like tuna nicoise salad. If these are left on the vine, they will grow into haricot beans, which are small white beans often used in soups. Beans add nitrogen to the soil, so if you want to try growing some corn stalks, they are good partners, as corn is a heavy nitrogen user and the beans can climb up

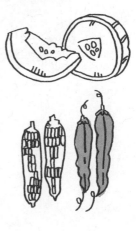

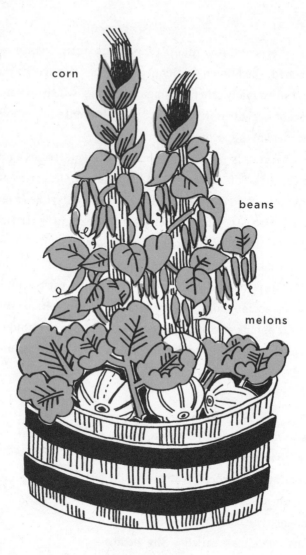

corn

beans

melons

whiskey barrel

TROIS SOEURS

the stalks. For small spaces, try miniature corn. 'Chires' baby corn grows on stalks that reach 4–5 feet. You can get about 30 mini-ears that can be blanched and used in salads, cooked, or pickled. Melons are good companions with corn, as they provide a ground cover that holds moisture in the soil. This planter is a twist on the Native American method of interplanting known as Three Sisters, which combines beans, corn, and squash. The chanterais melon here replaces the squash. This cultivar is a very small, supersweet, very fragrant variety that produces melons about 3–4 pounds each. Many people claim it is the best-flavored melon they have ever tried.

## BETTERAVES EN ROBE DES CHAMPS

Beets have beautiful leaves that can be cooked and eaten much like chard. The beetroot is best when young and about 1–1½ inches long, which happens about 55–65 days after planting them. They will grow until the first frost, so harvest a second crop after you pick your first one. 'Yellow Mangel' is a French heirloom beet that has a milder flavor than a red beet and won't stain your hands. As well, 'Chioggia' has lots of sugar, so it's sweet and makes the table look beautiful with rings of pink and white. Beets do well planted with shallots, which have a nice, mild flavor. These are ready to harvest when their leaves wilt and droop. Coreopsis, a native plant in many places in the United States, has cheery gold flowers and attracts pollinators and beneficial insects like lacewings that eat aphids, thrips, and mites.

radish

squash

marigolds

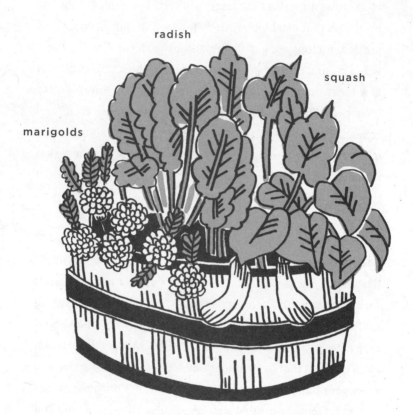

whiskey barrel

COUCHER DE SOLEIL NIÇOISE

'D'Avignon' radishes are also known as a French breakfast radish. Radishes mature quickly—in about 30 days—so after you harvest a crop, plant another one. These little lovelies are red with white tips and have a mild flavor. If you like a spicy, hot radish, try the French heirloom 'Plum Purple'. Plucked fresh and scrubbed clean, they are good served with the leaves on, with sea salt, local organic butter, and chewy brown bread for crudités.

Because radishes help to deter squash borers—pesky insects that bore into vines and eat them from the inside out— they work well planted with squash. 'Patissons Panache Blanc et Vert Scallop' is a French heirloom squash dating back to 1885. It's small and should be eaten when the exterior is seafoam green. As it matures, it has a white scallop with green radial streaks. Add a colorful bunch of French marigolds to this pot to deter beetles.

*Chapter* **4** THE SPACES
BETWEEN
BORDERS, PATIOS,
AND PERGOLAS

There are many ways of approaching the backyard, but one of the most important is to be realistic about who you really are and how your garden will be used. You might have big ambitions for the backyard, but work too much. I've had high-powered single bankers tell me they "want to start gardening" and think they can handle a high-maintenance garden. That's a disaster waiting to happen. People with pets and children who want fragile ground cover and musicians who are on the road a lot who want a raised-bed vegetable garden without irrigation are also unrealistic. It's my job as the designer to gently lead them to a satisfying but workable plan.

Generally, children do less damage than dogs in a garden. While people assume a child-friendly garden has lots of toys for them to play on, I disagree. Almost all my clients' children want to help when we are installing gardens—kids love the dirt, the tools, and the attention. My nieces and nephews insist on going to the plant nurseries with me, where they fall dramatically in love with varied plants; then, once home, they fight over who gets to put them in the ground. And studies have shown that if a child plants fruits or vegetables, then they will eat them. There is pride of ownership for the children, especially with a little extra praise at the dinner table.

Dogs can be hard on gardens. They dig up the beds, pee on some plants, and roll over the larger ones, crushing edibles with their boundless enthusiasm. Gardens need to be planned defensively. Outdoor lifestyle is another design consideration. I ask my clients if they entertain, and if so, with small dinner parties, larger cocktail parties, or barbeques? A friend of mine, Karen, who owns the business Urban Plantations, which installs edible gardens, relocated from Los Angeles to San Diego. When she and her husband bought their new house, the first thing they installed was a bar garden around the patio. She planted herbs and tropical fruits to use in mixed drinks. As she put it, "We really like cocktail hour at our house." Now there is a self-actualized gardener.

I once designed a patio kitchen in Sonoma wine country for a NoCal foodie. He's a real estate man who invests in San Francisco area restaurants, which is slightly more risky than day-trading. While this may be considered a financial folly, it's definitely an act of love and testimony to his affinity for food culture—it also keeps him on a budget when it comes to his garden. (During our initial consultation, he told me that he got shivers when I mentioned a living fence of espaliered Tuscan olive tree varietals.) You can certainly put high-end grills and wine refrigerators and whatnot in an outdoor kitchen. But little old ladies of Tuscany don't need a Viking grill to turn out amazing food. And when it comes to grilling, the ultimate in macho is the Argentinean *asado*. Once, while in Buenos Aires, I noticed a construction crew that had a fire going in the cement-mixing wheelbarrow. To my amazement they were grilling short ribs over it for their lunch. So use simple methods—an Italian clay oven, a South American grill on a movable chain—and add some real wood to your fire to improve the flavors. Surround your cooking area with herbs at arm's length, so that a fresh chimichurri or pesto sauce can be made while the meat grills. Simplicity makes this lifestyle affordable to many—and it tastes like luxury.

## A Kitchen Garden for Rock Stars

One of my clients is a rock star. Really, he is. I'm not going to tell you who he is, and as far as I can tell, his home life is pretty tame, but he tours a lot and he wanted a small kitchen garden. I suggested an irrigation system and a simple vegetable starter box. Have one planter approximately 3 feet wide and 2 feet high, and 1–2 feet deep. Place it in a sunny spot on your deck right in front of your kitchen window—preferably the one that you look out the most. Chances are that if you see it, you will remember it.

To make the most of this planter, there are three seasonal plantings rotated in it. The idea behind crop rotation is so pests don't thrive because you are interrupting their life cycle. Certain vegetables work well planted after one another. What I'm about to suggest is *not* for successful crop rotation in raised beds or rows. This is small planter rotation; therefore, you will have to dig around to interrupt the lifecycles of pests yourself. To do this, between plantings yank out the old plants and till the soil with a hand spade, a large kitchen spoon, or an arm with the sleeve rolled up; next, add some fresh organic compost. Start your first "crop" right after the last frost with mixed-green starts. Then plant your summer crop of tomatoes, eggplant, and basil. After this, plant broccoli, cauliflower, and Brussels sprouts, your cool weather veggies.

### FIRST PLANTING: MIXED GREENS

Visit your local farmer's market after the last freeze has passed. Look for a vendor selling organic mixed-green starts and get a colorful mix of red, green, and freckled lettuce. If you find arugula and mustard starts, grab some of those to spice it up. Beet greens are lovely, and when young and tender, are nice tossed into salads.

Plan on having one leafy green planted every 6 inches. Harvest the outer leaves for salad, but let the rest continue to grow. When the weather starts to turn warm, lettuce tends to "bolt" or start growing tall and narrow and getting a more bitter taste. When this happens, eat all the lettuce, add a little organic compost to the soil, and get ready for your second planting.

### SECOND PLANTING: TOMATOES AND BASIL

Back to the farmer's market or your local nursery. Remember that basil (see chapter 1 for basil tips) and tomatoes are good companions planted next to each other and come summer you can make a great bruschetta. A little later in this chapter are tips on tomato varieties (see pages 120–121), but generally

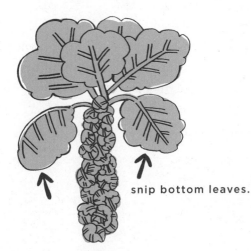

snip bottom leaves.

BRUSSELS SPROUTS

there are two different types: bush and vine. For planters, you'll want to grow the bush varieties as they get 3 or 4 feet high (as opposed to 6 feet); they also tend to grow out rather than up and their side-shoots bear flowers and fruit quickly. They may need to be staked for support, but they don't need to be pinched back. Depending on how you use them, you may want to grow a few different varieties.

### THIRD PLANTING: WINTER VEGETABLES

Honestly, if this were my planter box, come autumn I would just cultivate an entire container of Brussels sprouts. I love these tiny little cabbages. Throughout the winter months, I bake them with chicken, sauté them with bacon, grate them and simmer them in olive oil and finish them with a little vinegar. Stew them in red wine. Leave them on the stem and grill the whole stalk for a dinner party. You get the point.... Plant the starts when the temperatures are in the 60–65 degree F range, preferably about 3 months before the first frost. Add worm castings every 3 weeks and keep the soil moist. Clip the tips of the plants about 2 months into their growth so that energy is diverted from leaf growth into the Brussels sprouts. Other good cool-weather crops include broccoli, cauliflower, cabbage, and kale.

> In the Deep South's very hot, very humid summers, grow your tomatoes and basil when it's cooler in the spring or fall, and grow okra in the heat of the summer.

## Mistress Ginger's Tomatoes

I once had a client, a friend of a friend, who needed an emergency consultation, so I traveled to Staten Island. The building where she lived had six units with a front porch, but rather than a front yard, there was a strip of dirt separated from the sidewalk by a fence. Here, I passed by 'Roma' tomatoes in bad need of staking. The reason I couldn't resist this consultation is because the client, Mistress Ginger, was a professional dominatrix. Men pay her $250 an hour to spank them, berate them, tie them up, and scare them. Mistress Ginger explained her profession: "I'm like Mother Theresa with a fucking whip. This is therapy for the men." The phone rang a few times, and she commanded the client to get on his knees; by the second one, it became clear who should tie the tomato plants. The ones who like to get on their knees so much would be natural gardeners. "One of my slaves once made sauce out of the tomatoes," Mistress Ginger said. I imagined a lovely puttanesca sauce. The 'Roma' tomatoes would not go to waste.

**STEP 1:** Get on your knees!

**STEP 2:** Add compost to the soil.

**STEP 3:** Buy seedlings. Check the leaves to make sure there are no yellow spots or marks.

**STEP 4:** Harden them off for 1–2 weeks—set them outside during the day so they get a little wind and sun, then bring them back inside at night.

**STEP 5:** Wait until it's warm and nighttime temperatures run about 55–60 degrees F, then plant them in full sun. Full sun means about 6 hours a day.

**STEP 6:** Space your plants about 2 feet apart in rows when you plant them.

**STEP 7:** Stake your plants. Using wooden stakes that are around 3 feet high and 2 inches thick, pound them into the ground about 3 inches from a plant on its north side so that the tiny plant will not be shaded.

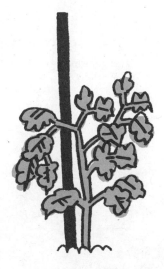

**STEP 8:** Tie the plants to the stake. Use cord, string, or rags that are coarse and bulky so the ties don't cut into the stems. First tie a knot around the stake tight enough to prevent downward slippage, then use the free ends to tie a square knot loosely around the tomato plant's stem. As the plant grows, anchor the stem to the stake every 6–12 inches, depending on how heavy the plant is.

**STEP 9:** Water evenly, with the same amount on a consistent basis, and water deeply. Every other day in the summer give them a good soaking, but aim around the plant so the water goes to the roots, not on the leaves.

**STEP 10:** Prune off stems that yellow or don't produce any fruit.

Tomatoes will ripen off the vine. Place them in a kitchen window so they all get sun. Turn them every once in a while to ripen them evenly. Their flavor and color will be much better if they are kept out of the refrigerator.

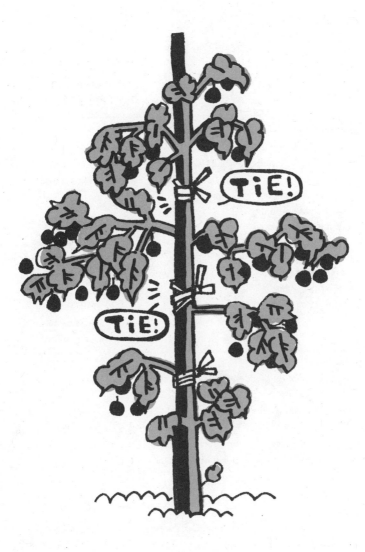

TYING UP TOMATOES

# *Tomato Varieties*

| TOMATO VARIETY | BEST REGION | PREPARATION SUGGESTIONS |
|---|---|---|
| **Stupice**<br>Early ripening heirloom from the Czech Republic. Expect lots of medium-size tomatoes. Bushy, but will probably need staking. | Cool coastal climate. Pacific Northwest, foggy parts of California. | Nice, sweet, clean flavor for a Tuscan-style bread and tomato salad. |
| **Roma**<br>Plum tomatoes that tend to ripen all at once. | Good for most regions. | These don't have a lot of water in them, so they are great for canning as paste, sauces, or ketchup. |
| **Brandywine**<br>Amish heirloom that is over 100 years old. Large pink fruit on a long, leggy plant. Needs lots of space and staking. | Very popular in Pennsylvania and Delaware, the Midwest, and other places with moderate summers (not searing hot, not cool and foggy). | Very versatile. Chop for salads, slice for a BLT, or roast with fennel. Make a coulis sauce and serve with red snapper. |
| **Green Zebra**<br>Dark green and yellow striped. Acidic tomato with a tang to it. Not an heirloom, but very good. | Developed in Everett, Washington. Popular throughout California. | Slice them for a tart made with goat cheese and mild onions. Good on polenta. |

| TOMATO VARIETY | BEST REGION | PREPARATION SUGGESTIONS |
| --- | --- | --- |
| **Cherokee Purple** <br> A large, lovely heirloom with purple tints that is sure to evoke admiration. | Rumored to have originated with the Cherokees, who are from the Southeast. Likes a sunny summer. | Great, smoky flavor. Eat raw slices sprinkled with a pinch of fleur de sel. |
| **Yellow Pear** <br> Teardrop-shaped yellow cherry tomatoes. Very prolific plants. | Cooler climates with short summers. Suited to containers. | Sun dry these and their flavor intensifies. |
| **Surefire** <br> Good, medium-size red table tomatoes. Developed to grow in very hot, humid summers. | Deep South, Texas. | Tomato chow chow or pico de gallo. |
| **Super-sweet 100s** <br> Hybrid cherry tomatoes. Very prolific; produce fruit right up until frost. | Small spaces, containers, hanging baskets. Grows very large if planted in the ground. Needs pruning and staking. | Let these ripen on a countertop and just eat them whole as snacks. Great dipped in humus, tossed in salads, or even roasted for pasta dishes. |

The tomato is both simple and complex, innocent and seductive. It is part of the nightshade family and until the 1830s, it was thought to be poisonous and grown only for ornamental purposes. Technically, it's a fruit, but it was categorized as a vegetable by the U.S. Supreme Court in 1893 so that the import of it could be taxed. It was also believed to be an aphrodisiac and was shunned by the Victorian crowd for this reason. In the book *The Historical Tomato* by Andrew Smith, he writes that the tomato "had been mentioned in the Bible. The Hebrew term for it was *dudim*, which translated into English 'love apples' or 'love plants.'" The author then goes on to tell that the tomato was painted by naturalist Konrad Gerner in 1553, who labeled it with the Latin term *poma amoris*.

Some varieties are open pollinated, which means that they hold their parents' characteristics and genes from generation to generation. Many of these are heirloom. A hybrid has a mix of parent plants and are not as unique as the open-pollinated ones, but are often bred for uniformity for commercial sales. But I don't knock them, as oftentimes these are developed so that tomatoes can withstand unusual circumstances, like really hot, humid summers or very short growing seasons.

## A Dog-Proof Loft

In order to keep my clients' chocolate lab, nicknamed Destructor, from destroying the plants, we ordered a prefab sleeping loft—this made it much cheaper than custom building one. We treated it for the outdoors by priming and painting it so that it would be weatherproof. We decided to go with a deep-purple paint. We then purchased vegetable planters to place

DOG-PROOF LOFT

on the top—two square ones at the corners for herbs along with sweet potato vines with chartreuse leaves and bright orange nasturtium to contrast against the purple paint. Baskets of strawberries and chocolate mint hang from the stairs on the side. In the space under the loft, we created a small, intimate seating area. Putting the garden up on a loft also created more space in the backyard.

There were two herb boxes and two planter boxes for greens and vegetables placed on top of the loft. These are dog-loft planter box suggestions for Asian-themed boxes as my clients were taking cooking classes from some of these regions, but you can certainly grow about anything that does well in a container here.

# Asian Mixed-Vegetable Planter

### Mizuna Japanese Green

This looks more like frisé than leafy mustards and has a milder flavor, but it is great for salads, works in stir-fries, and is a very nice green to grow in cool weather. It has a slight peppery flavor.

### Mustard Gai Choy ('Red Giant')

This is admittedly one of my favorite greens to grow. It has a delicious spicy flavor and is very tender in salads, but when the leaf is a little larger, it holds up to stir-fries.

### Baby Bok Choy

Growing "baby" rather than large means you don't have to space these out as much—about 3–5 inches apart will do. They grow quickly, so sow into the potting soil after the freeze. Harvest by cutting the entire plants off as soon as they look big enough. They grow better when it's a little cooler out.

### Pea Shoots

These are the tender tops of the pea vine. (Snow peas work great for this and thrive in cooler seasons and climates.) Simply snip the tendrils and growths off the plants. They are great in dumplings, steamed, and in salads.

### Japanese Eggplant—Konosu

These purplish-black, bite-size eggplants, when harvested young, are great for pickling or grilling on skewers.

In midsummer replace bolting greens with amaranth (*een choy hiyu*). This heat-loving salad green is often compared to spinach in flavor, but it has lovely red and green leaves.

## LATE SUMMER

### Daikon Radish

This cylindrical, white radish has a mild flavor and grows well into winter. I cut long strips of these with a carrot peeler and add them to an Asian version of a tuna nicoise salad, along with shitake mushrooms cooked in sesame oil and a tuna steak prepared with lots of fresh ginger; place these over garden-fresh greens.

### Chinese Cabbage

There are more than 40 types of Chinese cabbage. One of the most common is the heading type, 'Napa' cabbage. These have white tender leaves and pale tips. They are great cut up and cooked or eaten raw. Something a little more exotic is the flower Chinese cabbage, 'Nabana'. These look a little more like a broccoli and can be harvested just 40 days after planting the seeds. When picked young, they are popular for pickling.

### Broccoli Rabe

Translations on menus at a few restaurants in New York's Chinatown can be a little confusing if not humorous. I once ate at a Vietnamese place that had "Special Big Leg" and "Master Green Vegetable" on the menu. I ordered "Master Green Vegetable" out of curiosity—I wasn't feeling adventurous enough for the "Big Leg"—and got a heaping plate of broccoli rabe. Perhaps it earned this title because it's packed with vitamins and

If you live in a hot climate, grow a container of sesame. These plants will reach up to 3 feet tall and produce lots of seeds. Try a white, black, or tan variety. The leaves are used in Korean food as a wrapper for meat.

minerals. It can have a bitter flavor to it, so if you don't like this, blanching it in salted water removes this and makes it more tender.

### Kabocha Squash

This popular Japanese squash is green skinned and prized for its nutty, almost buttery-flavored orange flesh. Give these seeds or starts about 6 inches of space when planting.

### Lemongrass

This grass herb likes full sun and hot weather. It can grow very large in the hot areas of California and Florida and will keep expanding. If grown with other plants, it could crowd them out over the years, so keep this in mind. For people in colder climates, before it freezes, cut the grass back to about 3 inches and let it come back the next spring. Use it to flavor teas and soups.

# Children's Gardens

For children's gardens, I like to combine lots of texture and color with small groves for hide-and-seek and seasonal surprises. The garden should also have fragrant flowers and fruits and natural nooks for children to relax or read a book. Studies have shown that children will eat what they grow, so let them garden alongside you, starting seeds in the spring and then tending the vegetables. Many of the vegetables have once been featured in fairy tales and children's books, so read aloud *Jack and the Beanstalk*, *The Tales of Peter Rabbit*, or *Stone Soup* the night before. Also, it's nice to plant for birds, butterflies, and bees so the kids start learning about nature; many native edibles and beauties like sunflowers contribute to the experience. There's a method known as the edible forest (see page 135) that also works nicely for children's gardens. It's essentially planting an ecosystem that includes trees, vines, shrubs, and ground covers of all edible plants. This creates a natural sanctuary and has the added bonus of fresh fruits and vegetables.

## WEEPING PLUM TREE

Buy a nice size weeping plum tree from your local nursery. Dig your hole a few inches larger than the root-ball. Remove the tree gently from the container. Add a few inches of water to the hole, and mix in a teaspoon of $B^1$ vitamins (a liquid feed you can purchase from a nursery). Massage out the roots gently. If the tree's roots are really tightly packed together, then cut them with your tools. Place the tree into the hole, and pack some good organic compost around it. Water thoroughly, and then surround the tree with a bed of mulch about 1–2 inches thick.

cut-stump
stools

WEEPING PLUM TREE HIDEOUT

This helps the ground retain moisture, protects the tree's roots in the winter, and breaks down into compost.

Make sure your plum tree gets regular waterings and a good organic compost dressing at least twice a year. Any small shoots or suckers sprouting from the base should be cut away. In late May, when the fruits are beginning to form, look for and remove any rotten or diseased fruit. Then in midsummer, when the plums are about half their full size, cull out some so that they aren't touching each other.

After your tree has grown and the cascading branches are creating an umbrella, slice a log into small seats or find stones and set them in a circle under the tree. This can be a secret hideout.

## AN EDIBLE PLAYROOM

Plan a border so that your flowers are blooming for as much of the year as possible, and mix in nonblooming plants, like bronze fennel and lemon balm, for their leaf interest. Use nasturtium as a ground cover, and train jasmine up a trellis or tepee. Plant lots of heirloom pepperbox poppies in your borders—these grow up to 3 feet with bright red, pink, and purple flowers, and their seeds have a nutty flavor and are great for baking. You can also grow Hungarian bread-seed poppies that have the crunchy black seeds used in poppy seed muffins.

### Bronze Fennel

This has a thick stalk with bushy fronds that add lovely leaf interest to gardens. The bulbs are often used in cooking and have a strong licorice flavor—I love to slice them lengthwise and grill them. If not harvested, fennel will go to seed and bright-gold flowers will bloom. These can be plucked and

> You could also not prepare anything with your edible flowers, but just have the peace of mind that if your children stick them in their mouths, they will be just fine.

tossed into stir-fries; the slight anise flavor is still present, but it's more subdued in the blooms.

## Nasturtium

The flowers have a spicy bite to them, but clients of mine claim that their children love to pluck the bright-orange blooms and eat them raw and unaccompanied. Nasturtium is almost considered a weed in California, it's so prolific, but is much more timid growing in other parts of the country. It is an annual in places with deep freezes. Don't overfertilize it as it likes an untreated soil. When it is almost bloomed out and pods form, I like to eat the pods, as they have a spicy bite to them and taste a bit like wasabi. I make "capers" out of the seedpods by brining them in vinegar and herbs.

## Poppies

There are many, many kinds of poppies. Not only are they fresh, innocent bursts of color, but they are also often drought tolerant and self-seeding. The two best types for edibles are the Hungarian bread-seed poppies and the pepperbox. Poppies are considered a wildflower, and even these two varieties are pretty easy to sow. Rake open an area or areas where you would like to grow them, scatter the seeds, and water. Poppies will reseed themselves, so if you don't love them, be careful. While they won't necessarily become really aggressive like mint, they do tend to pop up in unexpected places. They also have very short lives, so enjoy their fleeting beauty for just a few days. Let the seedpods swell and dry; then harvest them by slicing and shaking out the seeds.

### Borage

This is a lovely surprise in an edible border. There are very few true-blue flowers in nature, but this one is a true-blue blossom with gray-green leaves. The leaves are edible but can be coarse as the plant gets older, so if you want to add them to salads, pick them while they are young. You can make a tea of borage leaves and flowers, which is said to help reduce the effects of stress—so parents, brew your borage. While the leaves taste a bit like cucumber, the flowers have a sweet start and a slightly grassy finish. Toss them in salads, garnish plates with them, use them to decorate cakes, or freeze them in ice cubes and add them to lemonade.

### Lemon Balm

Kids love lemon balm and will want to grab bunches and sniff it when passing by the herb. That's fine because it's hearty and edible. Make a lemon balm and basil pesto to toss with their favorite pasta.

### Pink Jasmine

Plant a trellis, fence, or tepee of pink jasmine. These vines can grow vigorously in warm places like Florida and California during the winter. Plant them where they get at least 4 hours of sun a day, and add fertilizer high in phosphorous. When the flowers open on the vine, the scent will make you swoon. You can add a

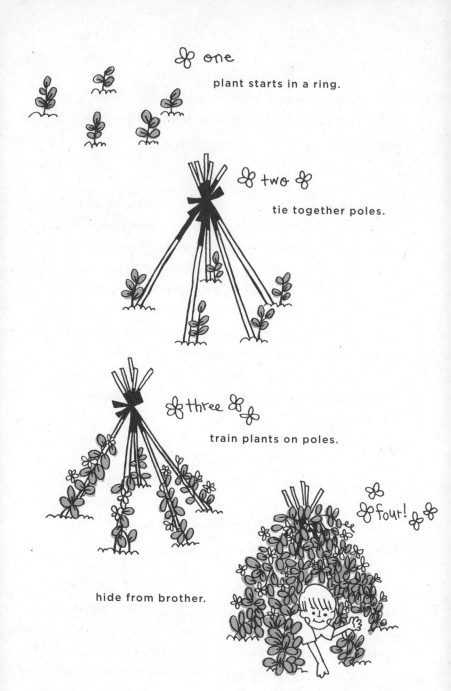

**one**

plant starts in a ring.

**two**

tie together poles.

**three**

train plants on poles.

hide from brother.

**four!**

JASMINE TEEPEE

The reason the spice saffron costs so much is that it comes from the tiny stigma of the saffron crocus. Unlike their brethren that bloom in early spring, these are autumn-blooming plants. It might sound fun to grow them at home, but bear in mind, it takes 70,000 flowers to make one pound of the spice, and it must be harvested by hand. You might want to stick with low-maintenance mint and poppies.

few beans to grow with the pink jasmine, and let your children sit inside the tepee. Pluck the flowers and add to scalded milk to make jasmine pudding or crème brûlée. If you live in a cold climate, keep your jasmine in a pot and bring it indoors for the winter. If it's growing steadily, re-pot every 2–3 years.

### Sunflowers

Place the seeds 2–2½ feet apart. You should see shoots in a few weeks, but they will need about 3 months to fully bloom. Since they can grow 6–8 feet tall, be sure to plant them in the back row. These flowers will literally turn their heads to greet the sun (a friend swore she saw a field of them do this in southern France and will never, ever forget it). Place them in a sunny, southern exposure. If you want to beat the birds to eating the seeds, harvest them as soon as the center flowers turn brown. Cut the head off with a 6-inch segment of the stem so you can hang and dry it. Put cheesecloth or a hairnet over it to capture the seeds as they dry.

# Lavender Honey Ice Cream

* *5 fresh lavender flowers and 1 whole fresh stem,*
  *additional petals for garnish, if desired*
* *2 cups heavy cream*
* *1 cup half-and-half*
* *2/3 cup honey, preferably organic*
* *2 large eggs*

 Soak the lavender blossoms and stem in the cream and half-and-half overnight in the refrigerator.

 Strain the cream mixture into a medium saucepan, discarding the lavender flowers and stem. Add the honey and bring just to a boil over medium heat.

**3** In a medium bowl, whisk together the egg yolks. Slowly add 1 cup of the hot cream mixture to the egg yolks, whisking constantly. Add this mixture back into the saucepan.

**4** Stirring constantly, cook over moderately low heat until the custard is thick enough to coat the back of a wooden spoon and registers 170–175 degrees F on a candy thermometer, about 5 minutes. Do not allow the custard to boil.

**5** Strain the thickened custard into a large bowl and chill. When cold, freeze the custard in an ice-cream maker according to the manufacturer's instructions.

### Lavender

This is one of my favorite plants. It's fragrant, it's beautiful, the bees and hummingbirds love it, and it's drought tolerant and edible. One of my nephews assured me not to worry about retirement; he planned on being a filmmaker and would cast me as a little old lady in his movies. For him, I make fresh lavender ice cream.

### Pumpkin Patch

Many people think you must have a whole field to grow pumpkins, but in fact a border alongside a home is plenty of space. Plant a pumpkin patch so that come October your child can carve his or her very own. These gourds need hot summers and lots of sun and space. As well, feed pumpkins regularly with organic matter rich in nitrogen. You can plant nasturtium and borage near it as they are great companion plants. Tuck straw "nests" under the pumpkins as they grow larger to protect the bottoms from rot. Choose smaller varieties like sugar pumpkins, which take up less space of course but also tend to taste better.

## An Edible Forest

The concept behind an edible forest is to create an ecosystem— a small forest where all the plants have beneficial relationships to each other—help to conserve water, and create habitat for wildlife. If you have a really large space, the possibilities are endless, with tall nut trees, understory dwarf fruit trees, shrubs, ground covers, and root vegetables. However, within a small space, you can still follow this general idea in a corner of

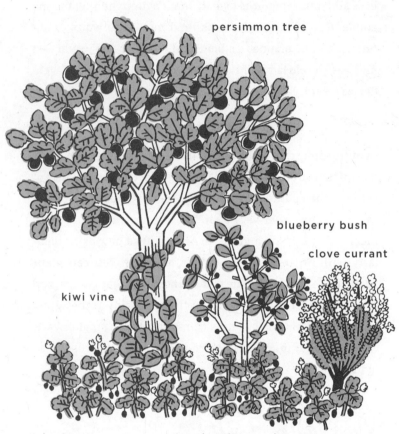

persimmon tree

blueberry bush

clove currant

kiwi vine

strawberries

EDIBLE FOREST

your backyard or even a small sideyard. Here are some planting ideas for a mild climate:

### PERSIMMON TREE

Admittedly, I purchased my first persimmon from a fruit cart in NYC's Chinatown. It seemed like such a perfect and surprising winter fruit—with a thick skin and pulpy center, a rich, lingering flavor, and a texture thicker and more viscous than citrus. Then, while visiting Florida, I found a small pamphlet of persimmon recipes that included persimmon pudding, tea loaf, dandies, fudge, persimmon sauce for pancakes, and (my favorite) persimmon butter for persimmon biscuits. But really, I like to serve persimmons fresh as dessert after a heavy winter meal.

There are astringent and nonastringent persimmons. I suggest you go with a nonastringent type, as the former, if eaten before fully ripe, can cause a remarkably unpleasant sensation in your mouth. Chocolate persimmons are collectors' trees as their centers have a spicy, sweet brown center that tastes like they've been mixed and baked right on the tree. (There are also cinnamon and brown-sugar persimmons.) They do best with a cross-pollinator, so if you can only have one persimmon tree, try the 'Fuyu' persimmon. These are disc-shaped, have a classic sweet flavor, and will grow about 15 feet high in the first 10 years and up to 25 feet overall.

As a cold-weather alternative you could plant a dwarf apple tree. If you're only planting one apple tree, make sure it is self-pollinating. Some of the most popular self-pollinating varieties are 'Braeburn', 'Red McIntosh', and 'Golden Delicious'. (See also the tree planting instructions on pages 45–47.)

### HARDY KIWI VINE

The large, heart-shaped leaves of kiwis are covered with a maroon fuzz, making this an especially beautiful plant. You need to plant both a male and female for them to fruit; nurseries have them labeled. They don't like direct sunlight and they are very vigorous, so they are perfect for training up a fruit tree. Clusters of white blossoms give way to kiwi fruit in the fall that is generally loved by children and an excellent source of vitamin C. These are best for areas that don't have a hard freeze in the winter, though there are superhardy kiwis that will survive. These are much smaller and the skin is generally eaten, like a grape.

### CLOVE CURRANTS

On the edge of your "forest," plant fragrant clove currants. These plants take heat and cold well, smell like cookies baking in the spring, and produce black berries in the fall. Prune these back in winter or early spring while the plant is dormant.

### STRAWBERRY (FRAISES DU BOIS)

I had my first *fraises du bois* strawberry at the kitchen garden of Robert Mondavi Vineyards in Napa. It's no wonder chefs in wine country covet these. The tiny fruits are packed with intense flavor—sweet but with a complexity that seems to unfold in your mouth. *Fraises des bois* translates to "strawberries from the woods." Another French favorite, the Mignonette, is an Alpine strawberry that is also diminutive and packed with flavor. Strawberries create ground cover for other crops and help keep the soil moist. They are also lovely, cheerful visual additions. These varieties grow in tidy clumps rather than on runners, and it's easy to walk around them to reach the other fruit.

# Outdoor Kitchen with Edible Walls

An outdoor kitchen can be as simple as a grill, but it's nice to have some shade to cook and eat in, so a pergola with edible vines growing over it creates both a practical and an intimate setting. Have your grill positioned on the far edge of it, not under the canopy where the rising smoke can cause damage.

If you're really handy, you can build your own pergola with some posthole diggers, cement, lumber, and nails; if you're less handy, order a kit that has all these as well as instructions. And for the least handy, hire a crew to make it for you.

You can greatly increase your growing area not just by training vines up the posts of the pergola, but also by running a board about waist-high alongside the pergola and placing rectangular planters under it. For this section I am listing small fruiting Italian heirloom summer squash and zucchini, along with heirloom beans and vertical gardening plants that grow on vines. You can use wire or string to train these on. At their base, plant beneficial herbs that deter pests, improve the taste, and help enrich the soil. I've also included an Italian heirloom tomato that grows on a vine and will do well planted vertically.

Adding this vertical gardening element to your pergola (or porch or chain-link fence) will create privacy and shade—as well as produce within arm's reach. Also, vertical gardening increases the air circulation for the plants, which decreases the risks of fungus, mildew, and pests.

### TOMATO 'COSTOLUTO GENOVESE'

These are thin-skinned and so don't ship well to markets or grocery stores. They are lobed and when sliced have deeply scalloped edges. These are favorites in Italy, but they're not

If some of your vegetables look like they are getting too heavy and need support, create slings for them out of old stockings. Cut a section off that's about 8-10 inches long, tie one end and put it around the fruit, and fasten the other end to the trellis. Mesh and burlap work as well.

common outside of it, so grow your own and slice them for mozzarella and basil salads or crush them into a sauce. They will do well in hot weather, but they don't mind a mild summer either. You can produce tomatoes for a long stretch of time. They like full sun and a rich soil prepared with lots of organic compost or manure. Stake them following the directions on pages 117–118, and when they are tall enough, train them over the rail.

### SUMMER SQUASH

As opposed to squash that ripens in the winter, needs to be stored, and has tough skins, summer squash can be picked, sliced, and grilled—just like that.

### COCOZELLA DI NAPOLI

Long and slender, this summer squash is a conversation starter—yellow with green stripes, it looks related to a watermelon, but with firm greenish-white flesh. Often, it is eaten when the fruit is very young.

### STUFFED SQUASH BLOSSOMS

If you want to harvest squash blossoms, get the early ones, which tend to be male. These have longer stems, good for a handle, and are just there for pollinating so leave a few, but they

OUTDOOR KITCHEN WITH EDIBLE WALLS

don't become squash. Female blossoms will have a slight bump that will become a squash.

### WINTER SQUASH

Zucca Tonda Padana is a striking heirloom that resembles a striated pumpkin. It is a vigorous grower and the sweet orange flesh is popular for making soups and gnocchi.

### EGGPLANT

This won't vine, but you should have room in your planter for a 'Bianca di Imola' eggplant. These have an elongated fruit and a white satiny skin. Slice them in rounds or lengthwise, toss them in olive oil that has a crushed garlic clove floating in it, and grill. When done, sprinkle them with fresh oregano.

Interplant herbs with your vegetables. At the base of the vines, plant parsley, cilantro, basil, oregano, and thyme. In the same manner of the French *potager* method, many of these improve the taste and their scent keeps pests away from the garden. These can be used for a variety of pesto sauces and chimichurri, which are great with grilled vegetables and meats.

### BEANS

Most of the beans you get at stores are bush-type because they can be mechanically harvested. Pole beans grow up runners and produce beans throughout the season. They also tend to have more flavor.

'Pole Bean Romano' are large, flat beans that have a nice flavor. You can cook these on a grill; they are terrific served with a light tomato vinaigrette sauce. For a shell bean, try the maroon-flecked 'Signora della Campagna'. Let these vines tangle up your pergola and then pick them when the pods are plump.

I tend to plant bean vines wherever they have a spot to grow—along fences or up small, spindly trees that aren't too shady. I try to get varieties with different colors and shapes. I find both their leaves and fruit really attractive.

# Chimichurri Sauce

In Argentina and Uruguay, chimichurri sauce is mostly served with chorizo, a fresh pork sausage that hasn't been cured and needs to be grilled. It is eaten as an appetizer. Once, when I offered to bring a salad or vegetables to a barbeque hosted by a friend from Uruguay, he explained to me that the chorizo was like the salad at an asado. At Latino restaurants in the United States, chimichurri sauce is often served with stringier cuts of meat like hanger steak. As for the rib eyes, down South, they don't add sauce. I like it with grilled vegetables as well, though this is not the tradition.

* 1 cup fresh Italian parsley (packed)
* 1 cup fresh cilantro or oregano (packed)
* ½ cup olive oil
* ¼ cup red wine vinegar
* 1 tablespoon lemon juice
* 2 garlic cloves, peeled
* ¾ teaspoon dried crushed red pepper
* ½ teaspoon ground cumin
* ½ teaspoon salt

Purée all the ingredients together in a food processor—or if you have energy to burn off, crush them with a mortar and pestle, old-world style. Make it one day in advance of using so the flavors have time to blend. You can keep it refrigerated for up to 3 weeks.

## Patio Cocktail Garden

When my friend Karen and her husband bought a new home in San Diego, their first patio installation was a bar garden. Since they live in a warm climate, they have lots of tropical fruits as well as citrus trees to choose from. Regardless of where you live, there are plenty of ways to grow fruit and mix a drink. Luis Buñuel Portolés, filmmaker and founder of surreal cinema, was also fond of his evening cocktail and is known for the quote: "If you were to ask me if I'd ever had the bad luck to miss my daily cocktail, I'd have to say that I doubt it; where certain things are concerned, I plan ahead."

# Karen's Eureka Lemon Drop Martini

The Eureka is a "true" lemon and is very tart and acidic. Karen tends to favor this over Meyer lemons, a hybrid that is sweeter. If you live in a cooler climate, grow your lemon tree in a planter and move it indoors for the winter.

* *1 ½ ounces Kettle One Vodka*
* *1 teaspoon superfine sugar*
* *1 Eureka lemon, juiced*
* *Ice cubes*
* *Granulated sugar, for dipping*
* *Twisted peel of lemon*

 Mix the vodka, superfine sugar, and lemon juice in a cocktail shaker half-filled with ice; shake well.

 Strain the liquor into a sugar-rimmed martini glass and garnish with a twisted peel of lemon.

# Micheladas

One of my brothers in El Paso, Texas, planted small Mexican lime bushes around his patio. These are small, bushy trees that work well for small spaces—though the branches are spiny. These small limes are also known as Key limes and West Indian limes. The fruit is smaller and thinner-skinned than most grocery store limes; their flavor is distinct and highly acidic. These are less common in grocery stores, as they can dry out quickly, but they make the best cocktails. My brother likes to use them to make *micheladas*.

* 3–4 small limes, cut in half
* Kosher salt, for dipping
* Ice
* Lager-style Mexican beer

1. Run the flesh of a lime around the rim of a beer glass, then dip it into kosher salt.

2. Squeeze the juice of 3–4 limes into this glass, add ice, and then pour a Mexican beer into it. (In some areas of Mexico they add chili powder, but I don't think *micheladas* are as refreshing that way.)

# Alexander Valley Peach Bellini

I had a peach Bellini once on a lovely morning at the Dry Creek Peach Orchard in Sonoma County and it tasted like California sunshine. The peaches were perfect and the sparkling wine was also from Sonoma. The most popular peach variety grown on the orchard is 'Arctic Queen'—a sweet, white-fleshed peach.

* ½ cup water
* ¼ cup (approximately) lemon juice
* ½–¾ pound white peaches
* 2 teaspoons sugar
* 1 750-ml bottle prosecco or sparkling wine, chilled

1 Purée the first four ingredients.

2 Strain the purée and then pour it into a pitcher (preferably glass). Add the prosecco or sparkling white wine and stir. Serve in chilled champagne glasses and enjoy!

When fruit starts forming on your peach tree, pinch off every third peach, or enough so that they will have plenty of room to grow and get large.

*Chapter* **5** **GARDENS GONE WILD**

FORAGING FOR FOOD

**F**oraging is an excellent option for people with limited or no gardening space. I'm trusting that since you are reading this book, you are a smart person who does not go out and eat poisonous plants. The best way to start foraging is to go with an expert—this might be a grandparent or a professional forager. These keepers of knowledge are often found through word-of-mouth or at festivals. Some foragers have businesses that guide novices into foraging. Chefs are usually an excellent resource as well. I've provided a list of foraging festivals (see page 208).

I believe that foraging is how life is meant to be lived. For whomever was responsible for creating the earth—God, infinite energy, Mother Nature—food was free. It fell from trees and grew on the ground and washed in with the tide. The world wasn't formed with coupons and cash and trucking produce from other parts of the globe. I truly believe our creator wants us to eat blackberry and hazelnut pie with scratches on our arms.

Foraging creates an interaction between you and your environment, be it city, suburbs, or countryside. There's a communion of sorts between neighbors who harvest each other's trees; along with appreciating each other, you come to celebrate the change of seasons. While some people bemoan the chilly rains of autumn or soaking springtime, mushroom hunters live for them. As you learn which greens are edible, what trees fruit, and where the berries are, your everyday experiences change. What used to be that weed patch growing in your sideyard becomes a potential salad or healthy soup; the branches hanging over the neighbors' sidewalk will soon produce figs, loquats, or lemons. Olives that are a pesky mess to some people, become Greek brined and coveted by others. Smelly ginko nuts are a delicacy if handled right. A hike in the woods that goes through berry patches often results in pie baking or ice cream making. And the spirit of the woods and the pleasure of the hike live on in jams and jellies shared with friends and neighbors.

And even if you don't want to forage, many of the top chefs around the country are all starting to use wild, foraged products. Artisanal products, like pickled fiddleheads, are showing up in specialty food stores. Art collectives are leading fruit forages in city neighborhoods and mapping out trees, and jam parties are becoming the new block party. Foraging is in style, and so even if you don't plan on going out to forage yourself, you are going to want to know what your waiter is talking about when he or she explains the specials.

There are some rules to abide by so that foragers don't get a bad reputation for wreaking havoc on a neighborhood or wilderness area. Many federal, state, and local parks don't allow foraging, but some do. Check with the park rangers first on limits. For example, at Point Reyes National Seashore, as of this writing, visitors are allowed to collect five porcini mushrooms per person.

Ask property owners if you can forage on their property. Most say yes. If you are foraging olives, they probably will beg you to take them. Same goes for mulberries. I find it a good rule of thumb to share with the property owners. If someone has lots of lemons and I take a bag and make preserved lemons, I give them a few jars of them. Tread lightly in the area. Stay on game trails or other paths. Fill any holes you make and don't cut or tear other plants. Clean your tools with disinfectant so that you don't spread diseases between plants (see page 60). Minimize your footprint—take only one shoot from several plants and no more than a few leaves per plant.

## Wild Asparagus

My grandparents were from farm families in southern Minnesota. My grandfather used to like to tell me that eating seasonally in the rural North meant having fruit and vegetables in the summer and meat in the winter. They didn't have refrigeration, and the Depression was in full swing for part of their life, so the situation created was the ultimate in seasonal eating. Since my grandfather was the youngest, he knew he was never going to inherit the farm, so he moved on. But he and my grandmother lived on a few acres outside of Kansas City and grew much of their own food. In this area, you can spit and something will grow, so their gardens did really well, some so

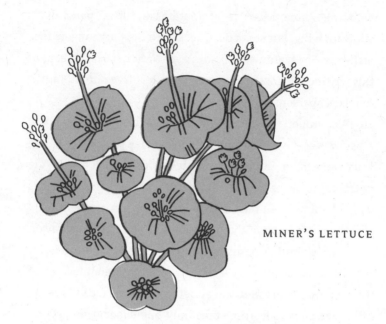

MINER'S LETTUCE

WATERCRESS

well they went feral. I have very early memories of walking the grounds with my grandmother, both of us armed with two-pronged forks looking for "wild" asparagus. It was a thrill to find a spindly stalk and chop it at the base. (Odd children, my siblings and I loved vegetables and used to fight over asparagus—though it was mostly a vehicle for melted cheese.)

Stalking asparagus was huge fun. The kind in Kansas had escaped from my grandmother's garden. Traditionally, wild asparagus likes moist, well-drained soil, so search for it near ditches; as well, some will hide out in weed patches.

## Miner's Lettuce

Miner's lettuce is a beautiful gem of a wild green. It's round and deep green and has a tiny white bloom in its center. It grows after a rainy season in big bunches, so it's easy to harvest. It self-sows, so you don't have to be too worried about overpicking.

In the purslane family, lore has it that it got its name from California gold miners who ate it for its vitamin C to ward off scurvy. Miner's lettuce has a grassy taste; when I use it in mixed-green salads, I consider it a "sweet" green rather than a peppery one. The plant is shade tolerant and grows in big grassy bunches, so if you grow it from seed and landscape with it, you'll have an "edible" lawn.

## Wild Watercress

This is a salad green gone wild, jumping the garden confines and reseeding itself alongside small creeks. You should look for cold, spring-fed streams. Make sure the creeks are coming from a clean source and don't have anything toxic or nasty leaking in them from a chemical factory or housing development. For example, if you find them in the borough of Brooklyn or anywhere near the Gowanus Canal or Newton Creek, do *not* eat them—unless you want to test fate and see if you grow a third eye or other super-herolike qualities. (I will eat fruit foraged in Brooklyn, but fruit on trees doesn't absorb the contaminants that leaves will.)

Wild watercress looks like its domestic relation but has a flavor that is peppery. It's a great source of vitamin C, calcium, and iron. Toss it in salads, chop or purée it, or cook it in potato soup.

## Dandelion Greens

You should have no problem finding and identifying wild dandelion greens. Ralph Waldo Emerson described a weed as "a plant whose virtues have not yet been discovered." People will gladly let you harvest these weeds from their yard. While the entire plant—flower, root, and leaf is edible, I'll focus on the leaf here. Harvest it before the flower comes so it's small and not too bitter. According to New York City forager Steve "Wildman" Brill, "They were even introduced into the Midwest from Europe to provide food for the imported honeybees in early spring." He recommends a second harvest in the fall, after the chill has tempered the bitterness. They are rich in vitamin B and beta-carotene, among a host of other vitamins and minerals.

Dandelion greens have a bitter flavor that can be balanced by cooking it with bacon or in a cream-based soup, but that sort of negates some of the health benefits. If it tastes bitter to you, stir-fry it with sweeter vegetables. I like to grate raw beet on a salad to sweeten it up at times.

DANDELION

However, you have to be careful when foraging these greens. Steve Brill, in his book *Identifying and Harvesting Edible and Medicinal Plants in Wild (and Not So Wild) Places*, writes about a time when park rangers infiltrated his edible tours of Central Park: "When I ate a dandelion, the entire Parks Enforcement Patrol converged on my group, and I was handcuffed and arrested for removing vegetation from the park. But after I was fingerprinted, they couldn't hold me: I had eaten all the evidence." When he was due to appear in court, he served "five boro" salad outside the courthouse; he became a celebrity after the charges were dropped and the city hired him to lead tours.

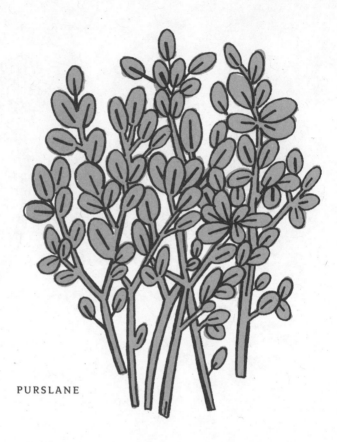

PURSLANE

## Purslane

This succulent weed is high in omega-3 fatty acids and vitamin C. It has small leaves that grow in clusters of five or six and are on mahogany stems that often trail along the ground. It has a sweet, almost citrusy flavor and is great fresh in salads. Purslane was used by ancient Greeks as a cure for the cold and for "female troubles," though I'm not sure if those were troubles imposed by or suffered by females. Still commonly found in Greek and Turkish dishes, purslane is mixed with yogurt, tossed in a green salad, or served with a yogurt dressing.

# Fiddlehead Ferns

These are a true delight of springtime. Ferns are usually shade-loving plants, so they are often found in forests. In early spring, fiddlehead ferns start to rise from the ground in small, tightly curled formations that resemble the shape of a snail shell—or as it's name "fiddlehead" suggests, the spiral end of a fiddle. The early blooms of ostrich or lady ferns are edible and should be harvested when 1½–2 inches in size and bright green in color. Only take a few from each fern; the fronds will not come back if you take every fiddlehead, and the fern itself will perish. Use them right away—wash, trim the stems, and cut off any brown scales; then sauté or steam them. (Don't eat them raw.) They are also delicious preserved in vinegar brine.

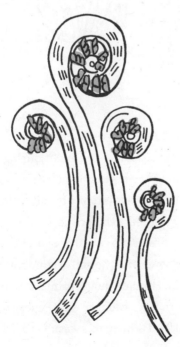

FIDDLEHEAD FERNS

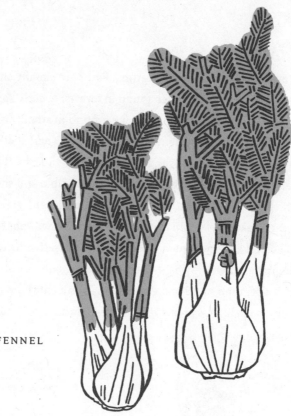

FENNEL

## Fennel

When I first moved to Sausalito, I was delighted with all the fennel growing wild along the roadside. One night during my first week there, I made clams for the guys painting my house and tossed some of the fennel flowers into my tomato, onion, and white wine sauce. It was a real "Under the Tuscan Sun" moment—until someone pointed out to me that Sausalito was historically a boat-building town and the soil around me had lots of toxins from that trade. From my housepainters' tales of their misspent youth and the occasional sweet smoke that wafted by during their breaks, I assumed this wasn't the first or worst chemical they had ingested. But afterward, I foraged well off the roadside.

Since fennel is often an invasive weed, I don't mind helping myself. In the spring, I get the base or bulb of the fennel when it's young. These have a mild licorice taste and are great grilled. The stalks can be very fibrous if not young and bland. Try to get them before they are more than a month or so old. The stalks are good diced into salads. Once the feathery tops of the plant start to flower, use these golden blossoms for their slight anise flavor and beauty—like in the aforementioned clam sauce.

# Ramps (Wild Leeks)

A restaurant in Brooklyn, Marlow & Sons, makes insane breakfast biscuits: flaky pastry with an egg, Gruyère cheese, and your choice of bacon or roasted ramps. When you have a vegetable going up against bacon, you know it better be good. And I tend to go with ramps, as they will go out of season after a few months, and bacon never does. (Better yet, cook the ramps in bacon grease.) Ramps are a symbol of springtime, particularly in the Southeast, and ramp festivals abound in North Carolina, West Virginia, and Virginia. But as spring progresses, they also are found in New England and the Great Lakes area.

> When collecting ramps or other plants with bulbs, always replant the "baby" bulbs that cling to the main root. Native Americans practiced this, and it increased yields of wild edibles over time.

RAMPS

Ramps favor the shade of forests and are found along streams. The overall plant is the size of a scallion, but the leaves differ as they are flat and broad and the bright green is tinted with maroon. Crush a stem in your hand—it should smell like onions; if it does not, don't eat it. Treat the leaves like spring onions, though some people get creative and make ramp kim-chee. The bulbs are often used like garlic cloves to flavor sauces.

# Nettles

I've seen nettles grow alongside fields in Alaska during the summertime, in woods in northern California in spring, in ditches in the Midwest, and alongside jogging paths in New York City. When you brush up against them with bare skin, they sting for what seems like hours. I used to hate them until I found out you could eat them. Steamed or boiled, they lose their sting and make for a delicious, iron-rich green. Just wear long pants and gloves when going nettle hunting.

NETTLES

# Nettle Pesto

Always steam or boil nettles before eating them, so they lose their sting!

* 6 cups wild nettles
* 2 garlic cloves, finely chopped
* ⅓ cup pine nuts
* ½ cup grated Parmigiano-Reggiano
* ⅓ cup extra-virgin olive oil
* Kosher salt
* Freshly ground pepper

1. To blanch nettles, bring a pan of water with a dash of salt to a boil, and blanch them for 1 minute. Remove and put them into ice water. The boiling takes the sting out of them, and the blanching helps them retain their bright-green color.

2. Place the blanched nettles, pine nuts, Parmigiano-Reggiano, and salt and pepper to taste in a food processor. Blend the mixture until smooth, scraping the sides occasionally. While the motor is running, gradually pour in the olive oil until well distributed.

3. Toss with pasta or use on a pizza. The pesto keeps for about a month in the freezer.

# Wild Berries

From Alpine mountains and meadows, to forests and bogs, wild berries are in abundance and such a pleasure, whether eaten raw and fresh off the bush or made into jams, chutneys, and pies. Once again, be careful of the wild berries that you eat and when in doubt, don't eat them. Take them to a local expert at a university extension or a master gardener program and ask. Here's a chart listing some of the most common varieties.

## Wild Berry Varieties

| BERRY VARIETY | BEST REGION | PREPARATION SUGGESTIONS |
|---|---|---|
| **Blueberries** Likes acidic soil, so does well in boggy areas. Fruits are not shiny. Five small blue petal-like calyx lobes at the blossom end. | Commonly found on the East Coast and in the Pacific Northwest. | Blueberry pie, cheesecake, or bread pudding. |
| **Blackberries** Likes sunny fields. Can be on canes in bushes or growing low against the ground. Many of the leaves are serrated and turn a rust color. Has thorns, so wear long sleeves. | Found throughout the United States. | Make blackberry smoothies with the fruit, and use their leaves to make a healthy tea. |

# Wild Berry Varieties

| BERRY VARIETY | BEST REGION | PREPARATION SUGGESTIONS |
| --- | --- | --- |
| **Raspberries** Grows on canes. Fruit often ripens in early summer, but later in far northern areas. Likes semishade and grows near streams. | Found throughout most of North America. | Make a raspberry tart with foraged raspberries and lemon verbena crème. |
| **Cranberries** Native to North America. Tends to grow in bog and wetland areas. A spreading plant that grows only 2-6 inches high and has evergreen foliage. | Grows wild from Maine to Wisconsin and down the Appalachian Mountains to North Carolina. | You know the drill: sauce. Dress them up a little by making a chutney with Indian spices. |
| **Chokecherries** Grows in shrub and tree form. Has white showy flowers in the spring. Fruit is dark purple when ripe in the fall. | Found throughout the northern Midwest. | Great in jams or dried, or made into fruit leather. |

# Wild Mushrooms

In a poem about the mushroom and changes of season, Emily Dickinson referred to the fungi as "The surreptitious scion / Of summer's circumspect." Mushrooms like moisture and often appear during or following the rainy season. There are three mushrooms that I can confidently identify and harvest: the porcini, the chanterelle, and the morel. I learned to identify the first two from an expert mycologist and commercial mushroom hunter in Marin County and the morel from my grandparents. To learn about mushrooms, there are mycological societies all over the country as well as mushroom festivals and experts (see page 208).

Learn to identify just one or two very specific, very obvious kinds of wild mushrooms with experts before you go out hunting. If you disregard this, you might eat a poisonous or toxic wild mushroom. Some are semipoisonous and you may just throw up a lot and become really aggressive. There are some varieties that Vikings used to eat to ramp them up so they could get their pillage on. Other mushrooms are so toxic you might need a new kidney, and yet other varieties mean certain death. So proceed, but cautiously and only after you've studied with a pro.

### PORCINI

I first went porcini hunting with Kevin, who owns the local nursery, Green Jeans. But his true passion is mushroom hunting. He explained to me that to find porcinis you look for long-needled pine trees near the coast. Optimal areas have these pines rimming a sunny meadow. You need some rain, but then these like a little sun to follow the rain. "I'm not a mycologist," he told me. "Just an obsessed mushroomer. But I'm pretty new to it, just been at it 15 years."

Mushrooms grow from a subterranean underground network of microscopic fungal strands called *mycelium*. When the mycelium fruits, the mushrooms release tiny spores, which are carried by wind, animals, or mushroom hunters; these spores germinate into new mycelium and eventually produce more mushrooms. Expert mushroomers with trained eyes can see these slight formations on a forest floor. Italians traditionally used sticks to poke "shrumps"—because they feared snakes. *Porcini* means "little pig" in Italian; it's a term of endearment for the baconlike flavor.

I uncovered my first porcini under Kevin's guidance and removed it from the ground as gingerly as possible. They are beautiful. The caps are a tawny brown color and the stems are thick and beige. They don't have gills, but rather a sponge underside. Kevin tossed me his mushroom knife. As he had shown me, I gently scraped off the dirt and when it was almost entirely gone, I flipped over the knife and dusted off the rest with the small brush and placed the mushroom in the bag. After this, as Kevin showed me, I buried the scrapings under the pine needles so that the Italians wouldn't know we were there—and more importantly, that porcinis had been there.

Most mushroomers carry their mushrooms in baskets rather than in bags, so the spores will scatter and spread as they travel through the woods.

## CHANTERELLES

A local woman showed up at Kevin's nursery carrying a gold-colored, oddly shaped mushroom and asked him what sort of mushroom it was. He immediately recognized it as a chanterelle and told her so. "Well, you can have them," she told him.

So along with her front yard, Kevin has a few local spots in groves of live oak trees that he hunts about once a month, after heavy rains. When learning some of his hot spots, he taught me that when tromping through the oak forest, it's best to stay on the game trails so as not to stomp on the beds. When discovering these popping up from the ground—not from logs—it's best to pull and twist them. It's also a good idea to brush the dirt from them at the site you find them.

## MORELS

Morels are a springtime mushroom, often found following the rains. These would pop up on my grandparents' property from time to time and were greeted with much fanfare. We would pinch and twist them out of the ground and wipe off any excess dirt with a small brush. You should use them within a week. A popular way of preparing them is to dip them in flour and fry them in butter. You can also grill morels, eat them alongside a grilled steak, or sauté them with spring asparagus in olive oil and a little garlic.

# Morel Duxelles

This is a great way to preserve morels for the dry months. They can also be canned and covered with olive oil for preservation. Preserved morels are commonly used in beef Wellington, but they make a great bruschetta when you serve them on toast.

* 1 tablespoon unsalted butter
* 2 tablespoons minced shallots
* ½ teaspoon minced garlic
* 10 ounces morels, wiped clean, stemmed, and finely chopped
* ¼ teaspoon salt
* ⅛ teaspoon ground white pepper
* 2 ½ tablespoons red wine

 In a skillet, sauté the shallots and garlic in the melted butter for 30 seconds.

 Add the morels; season with salt and pepper. Reduce the heat until the mushrooms start to caramelize, about 10 minutes.

 Add the wine, and stir until all the liquid has been absorbed or evaporated.

GINGKO LEAVES
AND NUTS

### GINGKO NUTS

Many people love how the ginko tree looks with its delicate, fan-shaped leaves, creating a dramatic outline to the sculptural tree. These ancient trees are considered living fossils and have been cultivated for thousands of years around temples in Asia. They are very hardy, and in fact survived the atom bombs dropped on Hiroshima. Because they are disease resistant and pollution tolerant, they have been planted in many urban areas across the United States. The only problem is the seeds from the female tree. These smell really bad when stepped on or when they get lodged under the hood of a car—some people compare their scent to vomit. So everyone orders male trees, but the ginkos outsmart humans; when there are far more males than females, the trees will actually change genders. And more gingko nuts get dropped. Foraging might be a lesson in serendipity. Once you peel away the stinky outer layer, the nuts taste like mushrooms and chestnuts—and are an autumn treat.

Matt Weingarten, executive chef at Inside Park in Manhattan, and a diehard Brooklyn forager, once spotted Chinese women gathering the smelly fruits under the golden leaves of an autumn tree. The women sell the nuts in Manhattan's Chinatown where they are purchased and turned into everything from congé to steamed egg custards. In addition to the gingko's culinary uses, the fruit and nut have been used for millennia in Asian medicine and could potentially help people suffering with all sorts of ailments like asthma and Alzheimer's.

Matt learned by observing the expert Chinese foragers. After collecting the ginkgo nuts, discard the smelly, fleshy outer layer while still outdoors. Once you get home, thoroughly wash the ginkgos in cold water. Let them dry on a tea towel for a couple of hours or until completely dry. Preheat your oven to 300 degrees F. Place the nuts on a rimmed baking sheet and roast them in the oven for 20 minutes. Remove from the oven and while still hot, gently tap each one with a hammer or the bottom of a heavy skillet. The thin shell will crack, revealing the sweet green nut inside. Matt serves these ginkgo nuts with pickled mackerel and a salad of fall greens, including chicory and radicchio.

OAK LEAVES
AND ACORNS

### ACORNS

Acorns are plentiful across North America as they are the seeds of 55 different varieties of oak trees. Come autumn we crunch these round nuts under our feet, often without a second thought about the gnocchi, bread, or muffins we could be making out of them. They are an excellent source of fiber, lower in fat than most nuts, and good for controlling blood sugar levels. Indigenous people used to grind them into flour and then soak them to wash out any bitterness.

Some acorns are bitter and others have a sweet, milder flavor—white oaks drop the sweetest seeds. You can taste them raw to see if they are the former or latter. Sweet ones won't have to be soaked, so you might want to harvest from one of these trees to save yourself the step of soaking them.

Check for wormholes, and if they look unscathed, pop off the top and squeeze the nuts with a pair of pliers just hard

If you want to forage seasonal wild plants and have a backyard, you can plant edible natives. Arlie Middlebook, of Middlebrook Gardens in San Jose, views this as the "ultimate locavore" movement, as you are not only growing your own food but also creating beneficial habitats for native wildlife while you do so. When planting with natives—edible or otherwise—she groups her plants into communities. There is the riparian group, which grows along streams and includes hazelnut trees, wild blackberries, golden currants, huckleberry, wild grapes, and elderberry. For a desert community, chia seeds can be scattered to create a beautiful wildflower meadow and whose nutritious seeds were valued by the Aztecs. Also from the desert community is agave, mesquite, and desert grapevine. You don't have to choose just one group; you can have multiple groupings in one garden.

enough to crack the shell. Run the nuts through a food processor so that they are coarsely ground. Then put them in a bowl and pour boiling water over them. The tannic acid should rise to the top. Toss out the water, and repeat this until the bitterness is gone from the acorns. Use a piece of cheesecloth to squeeze out the water and the last of the tannins from the meal. Spread this out on a cookie sheet and place it in your oven with the pilot light on—or in a dehydrator. Refrigerate your acorn flour and store it in an airtight container for only about a week.

You can use acorn flour to make pancakes, breads, muffins, and even pasta that is similar to soba noodles. Usually mixed with wheat flours for these dishes, it increases the nutritional value and enhances the nutty flavor.

Hazelnut trees produce nuts in the early fall, though sometimes they will skip a year. The wild hazelnut is smaller than the domestic variety. The jury is out on whether to gather them right off the tree or just after they have fallen to the ground. Either way, you will have some fierce competition with area squirrels.

If they are on the ground, make sure they have freshly fallen and haven't been invaded by worms. If you get them from the tree, they will be in bunches of two or three; pick them carefully and they will fall off the branch easily. After you pick them, spread them out in the sun or on trays placed in the oven with just the pilot light on. When they are dry, the outer shells will snap off easily.

Hazelnuts can be stored for several weeks at room temperature or frozen to keep them longer. I like to make a simple seasonal salad of mixed greens, wild hazelnuts, and foraged blackberries.

# Fruit Tree Neighborhood Mapping Projects

The three artists who make up the collective called Fallen Fruit—Matias Viegener, David Burns, and Austin Young—started by mapping fruit trees in their neighborhood of Silver Lake, Los Angeles, for a project for the *Journal of Aesthetics and Protest*. They did some research and learned that it's not illegal to take fruit in public areas and from trees that overhang on public property. They moved from mapping to fruit foraging parties that brought together 40–90 strangers of all different ages. These outings were followed by jam-making parties that all the foragers participated in.

I met one of the group's founders, Matias Viegener, and he told me that homeowners were often surprised to find out that the fruit was edible:

> They almost always encouraged us to pick more, and some even invited us into their backyards to pick. This project is really about connection—the picking of fruit and jam making bring people together in a playful collaboration. They get to know people they might not otherwise meet and the jam is a product everyone has contributed to.

Now throughout the country, there are specific mapping projects for neighborhood after neighborhood. (Though I have heard of conflicts happening when people tried to forage avocados overhanging sidewalks in Los Angeles.) Online or via a small community group, you can join a fruit tree mapping project or start your own.

### GUIDELINES FOR GETTING STARTED

Find like-minded people and collect their email addresses and phone numbers.

Create a hand-drawn or computer-generated map of the area you feel is within a reasonable walking distance.

Walk your neighborhood. I've seen unharvested trees in the sideyard of churches, on road medians, in the courtyard of restaurants, and in plain sight along a street that nobody has thought to seek out.

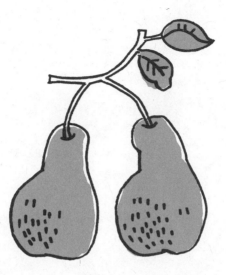

Write down the addresses and mark them on your map, along with the variety of fruit and its season. If the tree is on private property, always introduce yourself and ask permission.

If the tree is on public property, make sure there's no nasty chemical runoff nearby.

Start a website or blog to keep members updated: Make announcements about foraging events, list new finds, and exchange recipes.

Be sure to share with homeowners, the elderly, shut-ins, and other members of your community.

*Chapter* **6** **SHARING THE BOUNTY**

COMMUNITY GARDENING

While gardening can be a peaceful meditative experience, it can also be a social one, bringing communities together to create oases and learning centers in urban areas and encouraging neighbors to interact with one another in suburban and rural areas. Many cities are creating micro-farms and making healthy produce available while teaching job skills and building community. As well, there's plenty of room for collaboration and swapping in a community garden. Some communities are developing sharecropper programs where want-to-be gardeners are cultivating the yards of people who don't have the time or desire to garden, and they all share the produce. An increasing number of businesses grow fruits and vegetables around their office space—from raised beds in industrial areas of Los Angeles to NYC rooftops and Sonoma vineyards, they grow produce for the employees' lunches and enough for them to take home for the weekend. In schoolyards and at apartment buildings for seniors, edible gardens teach children about science and offer mature adults a healthy activity.

Garden parties are a way for people to come together and help each other install edible gardens, in the way old-fashioned barn raisings happened. With music, and a potluck at the end of the day, these events can have a snowball effect by recruiting more members to help with the next house. At harvest time, many people are finding that they prefer to can in a group rather than at home by themselves.

And, of course, there's gleaning, an activity older than the Bible that traditionally involves going into fields and picking the produce left behind during the harvest. It has been estimated that this passed-over produce can account for about 20 percent of what is grown. Throughout the United States, gleaning is enjoying a revival and has become a social activity. Churches, schools, and groups of friends get together to glean produce for charities. The food is donated to charities or to schools and summer camps for healthy lunches. As well, the media group Plant a Row for the Hungry, started by the Garden Writers Association, urges gardeners to plant more than they need for themselves and to donate the surplus garden produce to local food banks. Many community gardens also create relationships with food banks. At Picardo Farm, one of many P-Patch Community Garden locations in Seattle, gardeners compete to see who can donate the most produce to food shelters—and the results usually end up in the tons! To find out more about these groups, see the Resources section on pages 207–208.

# Community Gardens

Across the country there is a resurgence of community gardens, especially in city centers. In San Franciso's Mission District, for example, there is an amazing program called CHEFS (Conquering Homelessness Through Employment in Food Service), which is run by Episcopal Community Services. Homeless people are trained as chefs and gain job skills and the confidence to transition into employment and homes. CHEFS has a plot in a community garden where nasturtium grows wild, a cherry tree quickly gets picked over, and lemon trees provide enough for everyone. One person runs the beehive that helps pollinate the fruit and flowers; another member tends to the chickens that get let out in early spring to run wild, eat weeds, and leave their fertile droppings throughout the garden. Eggs and honey are shared with other people in the community, and in exchange, the keepers get plenty of homegrown tomatoes.

I've been lucky to be involved in helping run the garden plot for CHEFS. Rolf, one of the CHEFS students working at the garden, showed me the box where they wanted to grow herbs. It was a planting area that had been built up off the ground so that handicapped people could work on it. To make the most of the space underneath that was too shaded to grow many plants but seemed to have pretty good air circulation, we decided to give shitake logs a try. (Give a man a mushroom, he eats for a day; teach him how to inoculate oak logs with fungi spores. . . . ) However, a professional dog walker uses the garden during the day and the dogs pee on everything. So Rolf built a screen door to keep them out. We placed the mushroom logs on boards so they weren't touching the ground. They get watered regularly.

screened mushroom log area

ELEVATED EASY-ACCESS PLANTERS

In the springtime, we planted this raised bed with salad greens. To keep destructive insects away, we planted rows of chives alongside the greens, and basil and marigolds at the ends of the rows. All of these plants are so pungent that they deter aphids from infiltrating the tender greens.

While the students at CHEFS were great, we did have a problem with the dog walker's child—a little girl about 7 or 8 who was an absolute terror. She jumped in our planting beds and stomped on our plant starts, so we put her to work turning the compost pile and let her help us plant.

In community gardens, there are always going to be challenges. Problems arise whenever a group of people come together. But there are almost always ways to develop creative solutions, and that's part of the fun.

## Outdoor Composting

Clippings, leaves, and other organic debris can be turned into compost through micro-organisms and enzymes. This compost goes back into your garden soil and helps improve its vitality.

STEP 1: Find a corner spot for your compost pile or bin, one not too close to your edibles. You don't want critters to go from the old clippings to the fresh, newly sprouted plants.

STEP 2: Technically, you need no container and can just have a pile of clippings that will break down. But if you use a container, it should be dark colored, particularly if food scraps make their way into it. This will help generate more heat for breaking down the organic substances and deter turn often.

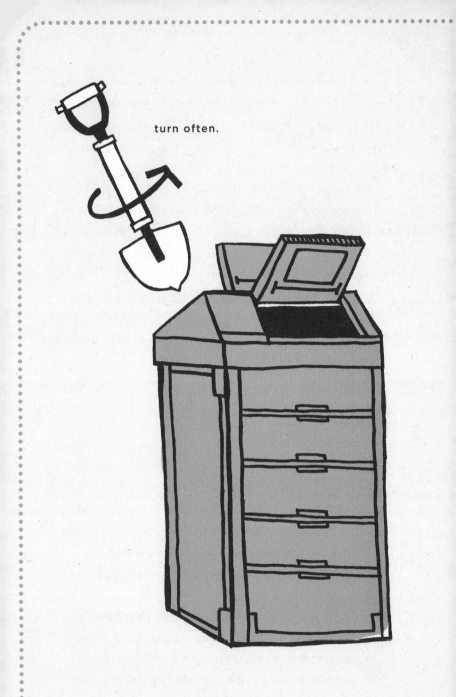

COMPOST BIN

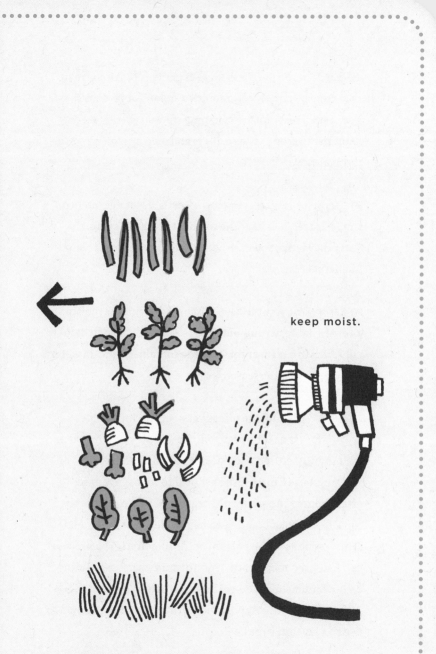

keep moist.

add kitchen scraps and yard clippings.

rodents. You can purchase these at garden centers and hardware stores; in many communities, botanical gardens subsidize them. I recommend fastening chicken wire under the container to keep out the critters and placing it on bricks for better airflow.

**STEP 3:** Layer grass clippings, weeds, vegetable kitchen scraps, leaves, and hay. The smaller the clippings are, the faster they break down, so be sure and clip large ones into smaller pieces.

**STEP 4:** You want to keep the compost with the moisture level of a damp, wrung-out sponge. This will happen naturally if it's in a resin or thick plastic container, but add water every so often if the season is dry.

**STEP 5:** Turning the pile is very helpful for the breakdown process as it improves airflow. So if your composter isn't manufactured and doesn't have a handle to turn or mix, then use a pitchfork or shovel to turn it every so often. Your compost should break down into a crumbly, topsoil-like consistency and have a clean earthy smell. (This happens at the bottom of the pile first.) The process can take anywhere from 4 months to 2 years, depending on how much heat you get and how often you turn the pile. Remove the compost that is the most broken down to use as a layer in your beds.

In late spring, a class came down from CHEFS' kitchen and harvested the greens for a tossed salad—fertilized with the

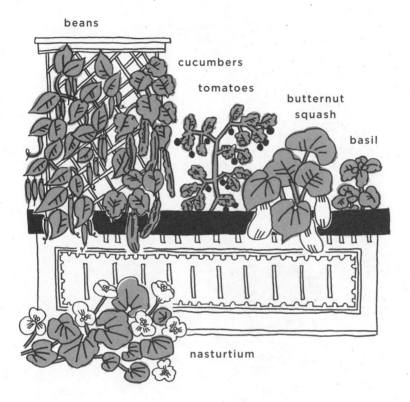

beans

cucumbers

tomatoes

butternut
squash

basil

nasturtium

SPACE-SAVING TRELLIS AND RAISED BED

community garden's compost—replanted the beds (with summer and winter squash, eggplant, and tomatoes), and made a trellis for pole and shelling beans as well as cucumbers. This space-saving trellis let us grow lots of vertical vine vegetables and left room in the bed for the other plants to spread out.

water
regularly.

straw

seed potatoes

compost

cardboard

milk crate

BOX OF POTATOES

A rule of thumb for harvesting winter squash is to scratch the skin with your thumbnail. If the skin cuts easily, then the squash is ready to be harvested. But don't cook it right away—give it about a week to cure.

## Box of Potatoes

Potatoes are resilient. I've heard tales of them growing in everything from sawdust to seaweed and of them tumbling out of compost bins—they aren't fussy. In a plot next to us at the community garden, people had created a potato tower out of used tires, but I can't bring myself to do this, as tires just seem so dirty and toxin-laden. So if you're gardening in limited space, try growing a box or milk crate of potatoes in straw and compost. For optimal potatoes, start by purchasing organic potatoes that have started, or have grown "eyes," to seed from a garden center. Days to harvest are 85–110.

STEP 1: Lay cardboard down on the bottom level.

STEP 2: Layer compost over the cardboard and dampen.

STEP 3: Lay pieces of seed potato in the box.

STEP 4: Cover these with 4–5 inches of straw.

STEP 5: When the plants bud, add another level of compost and straw.

**STEP 6:** Layer the compost and the straw until your box is full. Within 1–3 weeks, you should have green shoots spilling over and out of the top of it.

Place your box in full sun, which means 6 hours of sun a day. Keep the plants evenly watered. Potatoes are ready to be harvested in 85–110 days, or when frost kills the tops. If it does not freeze in your area, cut the tops off of the green shoots and wait a few weeks. This helps the skins become firm.

## Sharecropping and Yardsharing

All over the country waiting lists are growing for people who want a plot in a community garden. Many cities lost their community gardens to real estate development or just have far more demand than supply can keep up with. So people who have no garden to tend and others with yards but no time to garden have started working together. Sometimes these arrangements are between friends or acquaintances. But in some places, online resources are joining the "gardenless" with the yard that needs a garden.

One such group, Hyperlocavore, based in Los Angeles, finds such matches for people. In Seattle, Urban Garden Share is a matchmaker group, and on the East Coast, artist Leah Gauthier connects gardeners to donated land or growing spaces within the five boroughs of New York City. Everyone gets a little produce, including the local soup kitchens, and Gauthier hosts cooking performances with the veggies. So take a look around your own city for resources that help you find a yard to garden—or vice versa (see page 207).

If you find that a plant is unhappy in your yard—because it gets too much shade or wind, for instance—you can plant it at a friend's garden where it will be happier. I just had to give a friend my kiwi vines as they were so unhappy with the sun and wind here. She has two already but they've never bloomed as they're probably two males or two females. I gave her one of each. You want to know your plant is going to a good home, but sometimes, if you're working with strangers, you want to make sure you both share similar likes and dislikes. If you love beets and hate Brussels sprouts, you might do best finding a kindred spirit.

## Senior-Friendly Gardens

While gardening edibles is a luxury and a way to make the grocery budget stretch, it used to be a fundamental way of life for people. And many, if not most, of us have roots in rural farm communities—whether in the United States or other countries. By encouraging seniors to garden, we help them get good exercise as well as forge a connection to the past and sometimes a homeland. The flight of blacks from the Deep South is preserved in the okra and cornstalks growing in Harlem community gardens. Puerto Ricans have managed to adapt some of their Caribbean staples to the cold alleyways of Chicago, and the small Laotian community in downtown Kansas City finds a piece of the familiar in the summer garden.

The backbones and keepers of culture in many of these community gardens are the seniors. The many tips out there for seniors are wise for everyone to follow:

* Wear a hat and gloves.

SENIOR-FRIENDLY PLANTERS MADE FROM STOCK TANKS

* Don't twist into awkward positions, and especially don't lift anything while in these positions.

* Stay hydrated.

* Be as ergonomically situated as possible.

The best thing to help seniors garden is to have the beds raised as high as possible, so they don't need to bend and, if need be, they can sit in a chair. In this way, the beds are made accessible for people in wheelchairs as well.

One ready-made solution for this is to use the stock tanks that cattle and other livestock drink from. If you're growing seasonal vegetables that don't require deep roots, fill the bottom third of these with lightweight, nontoxic materials, layer over with landscaper cloth, and then fill with potting soil (see pages 45–46).

# Schoolyard Gardens

Since the 1500s, there have been edible schoolyards in Europe, even becoming mandatory in many countries by the 1800s. In the United States, the first official school garden at George Putnam School of Roxbury, Massachusetts, for wildflowers and vegetables dates back to 1890. Today, the sorry state of school lunches has inspired educators to start gardening programs that offer students hands-on courses in science and nutrition through their schoolyards. Helping to lead this revival is the Edible Schoolyard at Martin Luther King Jr. Middle School in Berkeley, California, which was started by Alice Waters, owner of Chez Panisse Restaurant. Schoolyard gardens are now proliferating with much success. Students at Nautilus Middle School in Miami, Florida, are cultivating different varieties of avocado

CANOE PLANTER FOR A SCHOOLYARD

trees, including some on the brink of extinction, as they also learn about the region's natural history. At Jones Valley Urban Farm in Birmingham, Alabama, even pre-K students are learning to play in the dirt.

Studies have shown that not only are kids more likely to eat veggies that they help grow, but a garden-based curriculum also improves their confidence in mastering science and instills in them a concern for the environment. It can also help teachers diversify their curriculum.

You can start seeds indoors for students to learn about germination. Once the seeds are ready, transplant them outdoors. You don't need a huge amount of space for an edible garden. One of my favorite planters is an old wooden canoe filled with potting soil and planted with herbs and smaller vegetables.

Visit the Resources section on page 208 for information on nonprofits that help fund and set up school gardens, and on curriculum ideas for courses in writing, botany, and business, among many other topics.

## Employee Gardens

Some businesses provide lunch for their employees. Some even provide bunkbeds, laundry services, and other essentials, but I'd worry a little about a job like that. However, a garden outside a place of employment does wonders for morale and motivation. Workers can take an occasional break from computers to weed and water, and then everyone sits down together to a nice lunch made with the "homegrown" produce.

I saw a great example of this at Farmlab, a place where art and agriculture intersect under an overpass in downtown Los

FOUNTAIN RE-PURPOSED AS A STRAWBERRY PLANTER

Angeles. I was shown around by Jaime Lopez Wolters, an agriculturist who designed some of the planters—old, reused agricultural bins discarded by California citrus growers. Along with these, junker cars are planted with vegetables and ornamentals. This seemed a natural for car-loving Angelenos.

In New York City, Curt Ellis and Ian Cheney garden in a truck bed to demonstrate that it's possible to grow and create access to healthy, fresh food in unexpected places. They recently converted the bed of an old green Dodge into their small garden of arugula, lettuce, chard, basil, and tomatoes.

One of my favorite vineyards in Sonoma County, Medlock Ames, also has a garden for employees. Along with being organic and pesticide free, the garden is an experiment in all sorts of new approaches to agriculture. Miniature cows and sheep wander the property to eat weeds. They've also installed hundreds of owl boxes so that these predators will help keep down the gopher population, and bat boxes in the woods help keep the insect population in check. They have goats who are supposed to eat the poison ivy but much prefer the tender carrot shoots in the garden.

When evening arrives, employees on the vineyard stop work and go to the garden to harvest 'Cherokee Purple' tomatoes, purple basil, melons, squash, radishes, beets, and Swiss chard. They also help themselves to raspberries, blackberries, and whatever else looks good in the garden plot. On Friday evenings, they often fire up the stone oven and make pizzas with ingredients from the garden. (Now this has to be good for employee morale!) There's no reason you can't translate this workweek ritual to a smaller space, and some of their methods (like the owl boxes) might work in more urban settings.

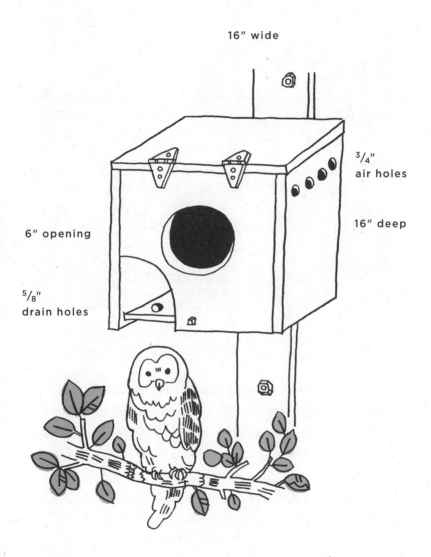

16" wide

³/₄"
air holes

6" opening

16" deep

⁵/₈"
drain holes

BIRD-OF-PREY BOX

The best rodent control you can have are hawks, owls, kestrels, and falcons. So rather than putting out poison, try mounting boxes for these predators in your community garden. Make sure other members of the garden are not setting out poison as this can hurt the birds of prey. Place these boxes strategically in your large backyard or community garden. Choose spots where they won't be disturbed by people. The birds like an open field to hunt in and boxes with trees nearby for protection and to help their young learn to fly. Don't put the boxes near parked cars, as the fecal matter is corrosive. Set them out in the autumn, giving the birds time to get settled before the winter or spring mating season. You can build a box with or without hinges, but it's easier to clean out an unoccupied box that has hinges.

Earth Pledge, a company in New York City that works with businesses, communities, and government agencies to adopt sustainable practices, maintains an organic kitchen garden where employees can pick produce for their lunches. They sit around a table in the elevated garden with views of the Chrysler Building and the Empire State Building.

# Gleaning

From church groups to university cooperative extensions, there are hundreds of gleaning programs throughout the United States. In fact, the U.S.D.A. has a toll-free number: 1-800-GLEAN-IT. Seriously, if you need gleaned food, have a second harvest for the hungry. Or if you want to get outside and bend and pick a little, gleaning is a great family activity and makes for a trip to the countryside—or big-city garden.

Some programs have extensions in many states. The Society of St. Andrews always needs volunteers, in towns across the country from North Carolina to Washington state. According to its website, the 30,000 people who go gleaning with the society pick up more than 15 million pounds of produce and deliver it to agencies that serve the poor.

Marin Organic is a nonprofit association of farms, ranches, creameries, and other businesses committed to sustainability in Marin County. For its Organic School Lunch and Gleaning Program, a combination of purchased and gleaned food from Marin Organic members is delivered weekly to participating schools throughout the county. Each school's purchase is supplemented with the week's donated gleaned foods, which offsets the costs, enabling the schools to choose local and organic food while staying within their budgets. The program supplies the food for more than half of the public and private schools in the county. The public wanted to get involved, so every Monday at 4 P.M. a group gathers at a different farm. (See the Gleaning Opportunity Resources section on page 208).

# Canning Parties

As more and more people grow their own food, canning, pickling, and jam making are becoming popular money-saving ways of preserving it. You can preserve your fruits and vegetables at the peak of their season and then enjoy them later in the year. Also, if guests drop by, you always have something to serve them.

Many people are finding it more fun to can in groups rather than alone. Some girlfriends and I forage wild plums in a nearby area, make plum jam, and later eat scones with our jam. Though not quite how my grandmother used to do it during the Depression, she would have if she could have. To learn the tricks of the trade, I went to a group canning session called "Yes We Can" and learned how to make dill and bread-and-butter pickles with Michelle Fuerst and Anya Fernald at La Cocina, the commercial kitchen at a nonprofit that helps low-income women become food entrepreneurs.

While some participants julienned onions, others sliced the cucumbers or washed the grape leaves and dill that would go into the pickle jars. This is a nonprofit project under the umbrella of Live Cultures, a consulting company founded by Anya Fernald, the force of nature behind the wildly successful Slow Food Nation festival in San Francisco. She is launching a response to the accusation that local and sustainable means elitist and unaffordable. She believes that cultivating such skills as canning, sausage making, and learning to buy and butcher whole chickens will help people save money and create more connections with their food, friends, and family. People can buy shares of the pickles or show up to help make them— and even those who were on early morning onion slicing duty were glad they chose the latter.

# Bread-and-Butter Pickles

This recipe is by Michelle Fuerst, our fearless pickle-making leader that day. She suggests that if you want to make them spicy, add a hot pepper to each jar. This recipe makes about 5 pints.

* *3 pounds pickling cucumbers*
* *1 pound onions*
* *8 tablespoons salt*
* *A few handfuls of ice*

For the brine:
* *3 cups cider vinegar*
* *1 ½ cups sugar*
* *2 cups water*
* *1 tablespoon mustard seeds*
* *1 ½ teaspoons turmeric*
* *1 teaspoon coriander seed*
* *1 ½ teaspoons celery seed*
* *7 peppercorns*

1. Slice the cucumbers between $1/8$- and $1/4$-inch thick. Cut the onions in half, through the root end, and slice into $1/4$-inch pieces. Mix the cucumbers, onions, and salt with the ice and set aside for at least 2 hours.

2. Combine all the ingredients for the brine and bring to a boil. Make sure to stir until the sugar dissolves.

*continued*

Drain and rinse the cucumber mélange. Pack into clean, hot pint-sized jars. Ladle the hot brine over the cucumbers, leaving a $\frac{1}{4}$-inch headspace. Remove the air bubbles with a chopstick. Cover and screw the bands finger tight. Process for 10 minutes in boiling water according to the instructions of the manufacturer of the jars you're using.

SLICING CUCUMBERS FOR PICKLES

# Edible Parks and Public Spaces

Fritz Haeg is an artist and the founder of Edible Estates, which transforms front lawns across the country into edible gardens. He refers to these edible lawns as "poetic provocations." "When people walk down the sidewalk and see these lawns," he says, "they're forced to examine the world we live in." This project has expanded to include growing edibles in a housing community in Austin, Texas, on rooftops, in front of museums and libraries, and in yards from Salina, Kansas, to Baltimore, Maryland.

In Irvine, California, an edible landscape garden dubbed "Farm for the Hungry" was created in a weed-filled easement. Its more than 80 citrus trees and numerous vegetable crops are tended by many volunteers in the community. Currently, an estimated 200,000 people are fed by this "garden." The city extended a bike path through the area, so everyone can pedal through and enjoy the transformed space.

Chicago is a great green city: There's an edible garden in the Lincoln Park Zoo where kids get to help plant, weed, and harvest. Also in the Windy City, the country's first certified organic rooftop farm, Uncommon Ground, has been planted. And the organization Growing Power has created an "Art on the Farm" urban agricultural potager garden where mentally and physically challenged children get gardening and culinary experience at Grant Park.

If you have unused spaces or weed-strewn abandoned lots in your community that could be put to better use, look into ways of turning them into edible gardens.

soak a cutting until it roots.

PROPAGATION

# Seed Swaps and Cutting Exchanges

Seeds might seem inexpensive and there are some great seed companies out there, but what if you fall in love with a plant and want to preserve it, breed it, or get to know its grandchildren? What if the seed company discontinues the variety that you love?

You can save your nonhybrid seeds for the next growing season. The ones that can be saved are the self-pollinated, open pollinated, or heirloom types—these grow seedlings exactly like their parents.

## SAVING SEEDS

There's no set agreement on how old a plant cultivar must be for classification as an heirloom; some say it's 50 years old and others date heirlooms to 1951, when hybrid plants were introduced. Generally, the term *heirloom* is used to refer to specialty plants passed down from gardener to gardener over generations. Heirlooms are also open pollinated, which means that wind or insects have pollinated them and then their seeds have been used to grow new plants that very closely resemble the original plant. Some plants of different species will cross-pollinate each other and create odd combinations, so gardeners need to isolate those plants if they want to preserve the species. Vine crops, like cucumbers, melons, squash, and pumpkins, are difficult to save as they may cross with other varieties and you could end up with a mutt plant. Start with peppers, tomatoes, eggplant, beans,

> When you buy a new pair of shoes, there are usually silica packs in the box. Keep these and use them when seed saving.

and peas. These can cross-pollinate each other and you'll end up with an *Island of Dr. Moreau*-esque veggie patch.

Not only is growing heirlooms an act of gardening and culinary preservation, but as well, you will have produce with unique hues and distinct and nuanced flavors.

To save your own seeds, let the vegetables get overly ripe. Beans and peas can be left to dry out in the pods. Then cut them in half, scoop out the seeds, and thoroughly wash them. Tomatoes will need to be put in a jar with water; let the seeds fall to the bottom and the viscous gel rise to the top. Then drain the water and dry the seeds.

Put the dried seeds in paper envelopes and label them. Place the packets into sealed glass jars with a silica pack to make sure moisture doesn't get to them over the winter. Store them in a cool, dry place and use the next year. Don't save seeds for more than one year.

You can trade some of your extra seeds with other gardeners. Whether on online gardening forums, in community groups, or with friends, seed swaps are becoming popular. If there's a horticultural society, arboretum, or public garden you particularly love, be sure to check into how you can get on its seed exchange list.

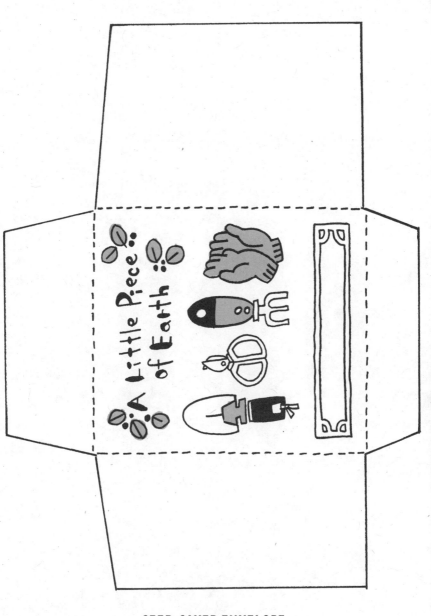

SEED-SAVER ENVELOPE

1. fold on dotted lines.
2. glue panels together.
3. label with species and date.
4. keep in a dark, dry place.

# resources

**CAR AND TRUCK GARDENS**
Junker Car Gardens: www.farmlab.com
Truck Farm: www.wickeddelicate.com

**CANNING**
Home Canning: www.homecanning.com
National Center for Home Food Preservation: www.uga.edu/nchfp
USDA Canning Guide: www.foodsafety.psu.edu/canningguide.html

**COMMUNITY**
American Community Garden Association:
    www.communitygarden.org
The Farmer's Garden: www.thefarmersgarden.com
Growing Power: www.growingpower.org
Neighborhood Fruit: www.neighborhoodfruit.com
Seattle Urban Garden Share: www.urbangardenshare.org
Southern California Yard Sharing: www.hyperlocavore.ning.com
Upstate New York: www.gardenshare.org

**COMPOSTING**
CompostBins.com: www.compostbins.com
Composters: www.composters.com
Cosmo's Red Worms: www.alcasoft.com/cosmos
Eco-Outfitter: www.eco-outfitter.com/c-22-compost-bins.aspx
Lower East Ecology Center: www.lesecologycenter.org
Stop Waste: www.stopwaste.org
Uncle Jim's Worm Farm: www.unclejimswormfarm.com

**DONATE YOUR PRODUCE**
Garden Writer's Association, Plant a Row for the Hungry:
    www.gardenwriters.org

## EDUCATION FOR CHILDREN

American Horticultural Society, Growing Connection School Kit:
    www.ahs.org/youth_gardening
Life-Lab, Garden-based education: www.lifelab.org
Literature in the Garden: www.jmgkids.us/index.k2?did=10397
National Gardening Association: Parent's and Teacher's activities
    and advice: www.kidsgardening.com
Real School Gardens: www.realschoolgardens.org
Sustainable Table: www.sustainabletable.org/schools/projects/

## FORAGING

Crested Butte Wild Mushroom Festival:
    www.crested-butte-wild-mushroom-festival.com
Mendocino Wine and Mushroom Festival: www.mendocino.com
National Morel Mushroom Festival: www.morelfest.com
North Carolina Wilds Food Weekend:
    www.wildfoodadventures.com/northcarolina.html
Ramps and Wild Leeks:
    www.richwooders.com/ramp/ramps.htm
Springtime Morel Festival: www.morels.com/festivals/
Wild Food Adventures: www.wildfoodadventures.com
"Wild Man" Steve Brill: www.wildmanstevebrill.com

## FRUIT TREES, VINES, AND BUSHES
### Berries
Hartmann's Plant Company: www.hartmannsplantcompany.com
### Citrus Trees
Four Winds Growers: www.fourwindsgrowers.com
### Espalier
Henry Leuthardt Nurseries: www.henryleuthardtnurseries.com
### Fig Trees
Wildcat Ridge Farm:
    www.wildcatridgefarm.com/fig-primary.php
### Fruit Trees and Bushes
Raintree Nursery: www.raintreenursery.com
Stark Brothers: www.starkbros.com
### Grapevines
Miller Nurseries: www.millernurseries.com
Willis Orchard Company: www.willisorchards.com

**Heirloom Fruit Trees**
Trees of Antiquity: www.treesofantiquity.com
**Olive Trees**
Santa Cruz Olive: www.santacruzolive.com
**Specialty**
One Green World: www.onegreenworld.com
Logee's: www.logees.com
**Tropical Fruit**
Pine Island Nursery: www.tropicalfruitnursery.com

## GARDENING/SMALL FARM INTERNSHIPS:
The Chef's Garden/Culinary Vegetable Institute:
    www.culinaryvegetableinstitute.com
Earth Harvest Farm: www.earthharvestfarm.com
Edible Schoolyard: www.edibleschoolyard.org
Family Farmed: www.familyfarmed.org
Lincoln Park Zoo: www.lpzoo.org/edu_programs_zip.php
Organic Growers School: www.organicgrowersschool.org

## GLEANING RESOURCES
Marin Organic: www.marinorganic.org
Society of St. Andrew: www.endhunger.org
USDA's Food Recovery State Resource List:
    www.usda.gov/news/pubs/gleaning/appb.htm

## MUSHROOMS
Far West Fungi: www.farwestfungi.com
Fungi Perfecti LLC: www.fungi.com

## PERMACULTURE
Permaculture Institute: www.permaculture.org
The Urban Farm: www.urbanfarm.org
Urban Permaculture Guild: www.urbanpermacultureguild.org

## SEEDS
**Asian Vegetable Seeds Specialist:**
Kitazawa Seed Co.: www.kitazawaseed.com
Swallowtail Garden Seeds: www.swallowtailgardenseeds.com
**Container Garden Seeds:**
Renee's Garden: www.reneesgarden.com

**Heirloom Specialists:**
Baker Creek Heirloom Seeds: www.rareseeds.com
The Cook's Garden: www.cooksgarden.com
Edible Landscaping Online: www.ediblelandscaping.com
Gourmet Seed: www.gourmetseed.com
Johnny's Selected Seeds: www.johnnyseeds.com
Kitchen Garden Seed: www.kitchengardenseeds.com
Marianna's Heirloom Seeds: www.mariseeds.com
**Herb Specialist:**
Rich Farm Garden: www.richfarmgarden.com/welcome.html
**Italian Seed Specialists:**
Grow Italian: www.growitalian.com
Italian Seed & Tool Company: www.italianseedandtool.com
**Organic & Biodynamic:**
Abundant Life Seeds: www.abundantlifeseeds.com
Seeds of Change: www.seedsofchange.com
Territorial Seed: www.territorialseed.com
**Seed Swap Organizations**
Blossom Swap Exchange: www.blossomswap.com/exchanges
Emily Compost Seed Exchange: www.emilycompost.com
Seed Savers Exchange: www.seedsavers.org
SeedSwaps: www.seedswaps.com
**Southwestern:**
Native Seeds: www.nativeseeds.org
**Strawberry Specialist:**
The Strawberry Store: www.thestrawberrystore.com
**Tomato Specialists:**
Gary Ibsen's Tomato Fest: www.store.tomatofest.com
Heirloom Tomatoes: www.heirloomtomatoes.bizland.com

**VERTICAL GARDENS**
Woolly Pockets: www.woollypocket.com

# acknowledgments

I would like to thank my editor, Chris Steighner at Universe Publishing, for being enthusiastic and intrepid when trying his hand at gardening adventures—both figuratively and literally. My agent, Jennifer Unter, is always a pleasure to work with and I am forever grateful for her support. Raquel Pelzel was an early collaborator and responsible for the section with chef Matthew Weingarten and foraging ginkgo nuts. I first started gardening with Lonnie Zamora, installing rooftops in New York City, and I couldn't have had a better inspiration or example for running a gardening business. Erin Combs, a fellow gardener in Brooklyn, has made installing gardens much more fun. I'm sure a few of the tips in this book come from conversations with Emily Hatfield, landscaper and gardener extraordinaire in Marin County, California. Chef and writer Kitty Greenwald helped with tips for not wasting herbs and Karen Contreras, principal of the edible gardening company Urban Plantations, gave me the idea of the bar garden. Thanks to my Parisian friend Karine Laval for creating names for the French market containers. I'd particularly like to thank many of my family members who are passionate gardeners: my late grandmother Vivian Stevermer, who had a fierce green thumb; my grandfather Mark Stevermer, who grew up on a farm in Minnesota and helped me realize what a difficult, noble profession farming is; my sister Betsey Finn, who has been a great collaborator with foraging and canning projects; and particularly, my aunt Kaye Stevermer, who has given great encouragement in my gardening and writing.

# about the author

MARIA FINN has written for *Audubon*, *Gastronomica*, *Saveur*, the *New York Times*, and the *Los Angeles Times*, among many other publications. Her essays have been anthologized in *Best Food Writing* and *The Best Women's Travel Writing*. She runs a garden design business, www.prospectandrefuge.com, and has a weekly gardening newsletter, www.citydirt.net. Finn lives in Sausalito on a houseboat. In her rooftop garden she grows edible plants in containers—amidst the challenges presented by heavy winds, saltwater sprays, and a pack of resident raccoons. www.mariafinn.com